Praise for *After*

"The journey from offered prayer to answer [...] one. The trail is fraught with shadows an[...] moving in the right direction. Rusty George offers it. His engaging style will warm your heart. His careful interpretation of Scripture will lift your faith. This book will help you navigate the path. Read it, and take heart. God has heard your prayers."

> —**Max Lucado,** best-selling author of *Anxious for Nothing* and *Before Amen*

"A needed insight into the questions so many of us have: Does God really hear my prayers? And if so, why does it feel like nothing is happening? *After Amen* provides important next steps for us while we wait on God's answer."

> —**Mark Batterson,** *New York Times* best-selling author of *The Circle Maker* and lead pastor of National Community Church

"Whether you're a Jesus follower or you just watch from a distance, Rusty tackles questions many of us have. Rusty's insights are timely and so needed today."

> —**Andy Stanley,** pastor at North Point Community Church, best-selling author, and founder of North Point Ministries

"Praying doesn't take that long. And it seems too simple. What comes next? Waiting. In *After Amen*, my friend Rusty teaches us how to wait courageously with humility, hope, and so much more. Wait no longer— read this book."

> —**Kyle Idleman,** senior pastor at Southeast Christian Church and author of *Not a Fan* and *Don't Give Up*

"Rusty's latest book is a beautiful encouragement for when we wonder if heaven is hearing our voices."

> —**Bob Goff**, *New York Times* best-selling author of *Love Does* and *Everybody Always*

"Rusty wrestles with common questions and doubts about prayer, then walks you through what it looks like to live out a dynamic, thriving relationship with God through prayer."

> —**Carey Nieuwhof,** best-selling author of *Didn't See It Coming* and founding pastor of Connexus Church

"Rusty's prayers and insights are rooted in both honesty and a deep knowledge of the character of God. Read this, and you will find your prayer life blessed and transformed like never before."

—**Randy Frazee,** pastor and author of *What Happens after You Die*

"Uncertain seasons are hardly ever enjoyable, but they don't have to be unbearable. As Rusty reminds us, intentional prayer can guide us through the toughest of circumstances . . . and we might even learn some lessons along the way and be stronger for it."

—**Caleb Kaltenbach,** director of The Messy Grace Group and author of *Messy Grace* and *God of Tomorrow*

"If you've ever had questions about prayer, this book is a must-read. Through his personal stories and deep insight, Rusty George will give you a fresh perspective not only on what it means to pray but also what it means to proactively wait after you say amen."

—**Kristina Kuzmic,** author of *Hold On, but Don't Hold Still*

"A raw, relatable, and relevant book that leaders today so desperately need."

—**Brad Lomenick,** founder of BLINC and author of *H3 Leadership* and *The Catalyst Leader*

"*After Amen* is helpful, honest, relatable, and hopeful! If you are wondering about God, waiting on God, frustrated with God—read this book!"

—**Jodi Hickerson,** Mission Church

"Rusty George has delivered a true blessing for us all with *After Amen*, a book with biblical principles, humor, practical applications, and a real guide that can help us pray and wait patiently in a way we never thought possible."

—**Dan Angel,** producer of the award-winning films *Gifted Hands* and *Door to Door*

"*After Amen* is *not* a good book. It is a *great* conversation. Reading *After Amen* is like sitting across the coffee table from Rusty as he unpacks his own path to prayer. He will vulnerably lead you to prayer proficiency."

—**Mark E. Moore,** author of *Core52*

"Rusty's books have all been informative, inspirational, and life-changing. *After Amen* is another great addition and a must-read for any who find themselves wondering if God hears their prayers!"

—**Kevan Miller,** professional hockey player with the Boston Bruins

"A sacred space exists after we utter amen. A space filled with silence. A space filled with anxiety. A space filled with insecurities, anger, agitation, and spiritual growth. In *After Amen*, Rusty George pastorally presses into this sacred space, offering practical wisdom and scriptural supervision."

—**Shane J. Wood,** professor of New Testament Studies at Ozark Christian College and author of *Between Two Trees*

"Rusty helps us navigate the awkward seasons of silence when we've stopped talking, but God hasn't started. With humor and the heart of a pastor, Rusty breaks these seasons into bite-sized chunks that help provide the breakthrough we all seek."

—**Lane Jones,** North Point Ministries

"Rusty communicates his message with insight, humor, and—most importantly—heart! As a Christian who struggles with many aspects of prayer, reading *After Amen* was a much-needed dose of novel clarity and encouragement on what can be a very obtuse subject."

—**Chris Dowling,** director of *Run the Race* and *Where Hope Grows*

"Rusty George is hilarious, real, and wise. If you've ever had a prayer not answered and wondered why, this is the book you've been waiting for!"

—**Vince Antonucci,** pastor of Verve Church and author of *Restore*

"Rusty has a unique way of communicating God's truth that will have you laughing one minute and convicted the next. By the time you put this book down, your view of prayer will be transformed as well as your prayer life."

—**Shane Philip,** senior pastor of The Crossing Church

"What happens after amen? Do our requests even get heard? Do they seem trivial to a very busy God? Can you use up all your data or are there unlimited minutes? Rusty wades into these very real questions with honesty, clarity, humor, and fresh insight."

—**Mike Breaux,** pastor, Ventura, California

"A raw and relatable book that the church today so desperately needs. Rusty's prayers and insights are rooted in both honesty and a deep knowledge of the character of God. Read this, and you will find your prayer life blessed and transformed like never before."

—**Gene Appel,** senior pastor, Eastside Christian Church, Anaheim, California

"When I was in seminary, I wanted to 'figure prayer out.' So, I read several books by people with letters after their names. I sure wish I had read Rusty's book back then. I got a lot more out of it, and it was much funnier than the others!"

—**Todd Elliot,** lead pastor of Beach Church

"I have read all of Rusty's books, and I love them all, but this might be the best one. *After Amen* is engaging, thought-provoking, and funny! You will be glad you read this book!"

—**Mark Weigt,** lead pastor at The Ridge Community Church

"If you've ever wondered why God seems to answer some prayers and not others, and what you're supposed to do when your prayers are the ones he's not answering, this book is for you. With transparency, wit, and genuine biblical insight, Rusty George tackles this most powerful aspect of our walk with Jesus."

—**Larry Osborne,** pastor of North Coast Church and author of
Thriving in Babylon

"I had the privilege of reading *After Amen* during the height of the coronavirus pandemic. *After Amen* not only instructed me in the fundamentals of prayer during that difficult season; its principles guided me. If you are going through troubling times and wondering where God is or whether he even cares, *After Amen* is a resource you can't do without."

—**Brian Dodd,** author, blogger, and Injoy Stewardship Ministry director

"Rusty is wise, hilarious, and honest. You'll find yourself laughing out loud and transformed from the inside out."

—**Dave Dummitt,** lead pastor at Willow Creek Community Church

"Rusty answers the questions you've been asking about prayer as well as many others you wish you'd asked! Settle in and enjoy!"

—**Jan Johnson,** author of *When the Soul Listens* and
Meeting God in Scripture

"Rusty has, once again, written a relevant and timely book that gives helpful direction on how to deal with an age-old struggle. His mix of humor, insight, and experience guides any reader through the often-confusing waters of prayers offered to an invisible God."

—**Rob McDowell,** lead pastor at North Metro Church

After
Amen

● ● ●

What to Do When You're
Waiting on God

RUSTY GEORGE

LEAFWOOD
PUBLISHERS
an imprint of Abilene Christian University Press

AFTER AMEN

What to Do When You're Waiting on God

LEAFWOOD
P U B L I S H E R S

an imprint of Abilene Christian University Press

Copyright © 2020 by Rusty George

ISBN 978-1-68426-081-2 | LCCN 2020014399

Printed in the United States of America

Published in association with The Gates Group, 1403 Walnut Lane, Louisville, KY 40223

LIBRARY OF CONGRESS CATALOGING-IN-PUBLICATION DATA
Names: George, Rusty, 1971- author.
Title: After amen : what to do when you're waiting on God / Rusty George.
Description: Abilene, Texas : Leafwood Publishers, 2020.
Identifiers: LCCN 2020014398 (print) | LCCN 2020014399 (ebook) | ISBN
    9781684260812 (paperback) | ISBN 9781684269563 (epub)
Subjects: LCSH: Prayer—Christianity. | Waiting (Philosophy) | Expectation
    (Psychology—Religious aspects--Christianity.
Classification: LCC BV220 .G46 2020 (print) | LCC BV220 (ebook) | DDC 248.3/2—dc23
LC record available at https://lccn.loc.gov/2020014398
LC ebook record available at https://lccn.loc.gov/2020014399

Cover design by Bruce Gore | Gore Studio, Inc. | Interior text design by Sandy Armstrong, Strong Design

Leafwood Publishers is an imprint of Abilene Christian University Press
ACU Box 29138, Abilene, Texas 79699

1-877-816-4455 | www.leafwoodpublishers.com

20 21 22 23 24 25 / 7 6 5 4 3 2 1

For my mom, Mary George,
my first prayer warrior.
Thanks for all the years you have sat
in the "waiting room" on my behalf.

Contents

Hello?
Is Anybody Out There?

We are dog people.

I know others like cats, and my kids would love that, but since a couple of us are allergic to cats, we are dog people.

That being said, my youngest daughter, Sidney, was scared of dogs until she was around four years old. That is when she met a Shih Tzu puppy named Charlie Brown. Our friend Jill had a Shih Tzu that had puppies, and Charlie Brown was one of them. He was cute, cuddly, soft, and had markings on his back like Charlie Brown's famous T-shirt—thus his name. And Sidney fell in love. We all did, to be honest. So we decided if we were going to get a dog, we should get this one because Sidney wasn't scared of him.

My wife and I had had dogs before, but we had never had a Shih Tzu. We were amazed at how great a dog this one was. Charlie was fun, trainable, and as calm as a puppy can be. And as time went by, Charlie only got better. Personable, loyal, photogenic—all the qualities of a great dog. So, years later, when Jill called to tell us that Charlie's mom was expecting another litter, we thought, *What's better than one dog? Two!* We told Jill if there were a girl pup, we'd take her. Not a boy. We didn't want the Alpha Dog battle in our home; but a girl . . . that would be perfect. Our girls were eight and ten at the time, so they were perfectly suited to help take care of the added dog. Jill said, "Well, I have one girl promised already, so if we have girls, the second one is yours." Deal.

We began the waiting process to see if Charlie would be getting a sister. Picking a name was easy. We had to go with Lucy, of course. Barring any incident with a football, these two should be a perfect pair. The waiting was the tough part. Our girls were so excited, as were we, but we tried to be realistic. We kept telling our kids that there might not be two girls, so we shouldn't get our hopes up. But you know, telling your kids to not get their hopes up regarding a possible puppy is like telling them to go to sleep early on Christmas Eve.

One August evening, we got the call around dinnertime. Momma dog was in labor. The puppies were on their way. We would soon learn the verdict. We waited—not so patiently—for the up-to-the-minute results coming in via text. Buzz. "First puppy: it's a girl!" *Perfect. Now the next girl is ours.* Buzz. "Second puppy: it's a boy." *Okay, we can live with that. Surely, she'll have more.* Buzz. "Third puppy: it's a boy." *Hmm. Now we're getting nervous.* And then the texts stopped. After about thirty minutes, we finally got one last text: "Sorry . . . I think that's it." We were all devastated. My wife, Lorrie, and I knew that we had to put on a tough face: "It's okay, maybe we'll get another one somewhere else." "Let's just be happy with what we have." And other frustrated phrases like that.

However, the really interesting comments happened next. Through tears, I heard Lindsey, our ten-year-old, say, "I don't know why this happened. I've been praying for this!" Then, almost confessing, my eight-year-old daughter, Sidney, said, "It's all my fault. I didn't pray at all." Lindsey looked at Sidney like she was holding a bag of thirty pieces of silver.

What do you say as a parent? How do you deal with this theological conundrum?

Did Sidney cause the dog not to have another girl by not praying? Did God say no to Lindsey? Was any of this even God's fault? I know God cares about people, but did God really care about how many puppies there would be?

I answered them the way any parent would: "Girls, it's time for bed."

Lorrie and I finally got the girls calmed down that fateful night and put them to bed. But not long after they went to sleep, we got another text from Jill. She said, "We've got one more puppy. It came late! And it's a girl!"

We were so excited that we couldn't wait till morning. I rushed into the girls' bedroom and yelled, "She had another puppy—and it's a girl! The girls sat up, stunned, said okay, and fell back asleep. Not quite the reaction I was envisioning. The next morning, I asked if they remembered me coming into their room last night. "No, Dad." So, I told them the good news again, and I finally got the reaction I was expecting. There was great rejoicing. Lindsey felt her prayers had been answered. Sidney felt her lack of prayers had been forgiven. And Lorrie and I were thrilled to see them so happy.

You and I have prayed for much more than just a puppy, but we have had the same questions about God and prayer. Every day, we join the throngs of billions as we beg God for his help.

A family prays for a parent to be free from cancer.

A couple prays for a pregnancy.

A child prays for her parents to stop fighting and not separate.

A church prays for God to move in their city.

A pastor prays for his congregation to get serious about following Jesus.

We've all prayed big prayers only to hear nothing.

So we are left with our questions: Why does God seem to answer some prayers and not others? Do my actions determine his answers? Is he waiting on me to do something? Should I even keep asking?

We Question God's Decision Making

Why did God say no? And why does he say yes to some yet no to me?

I walked with a man through the darkest of days. He lost a custody hearing to his ex-wife, whose boyfriend had molested my friend's children. We prayed for months for God to help the judge see the truth and award these precious children to the safety of their father. But the judge said no. But why? Why did God do nothing?

The only thing worse than God's silence is when I hear others celebrate what they believe God has done for them. For example: "I was at the mall, it was packed, and I prayed for a parking spot. Just then, a car backed out of a front row space. Praise God!" Seriously?

This causes us to question if God is great and able. Is he good and willing? Why would he allow this? And if I throw out his activity in the parking spot, do I need to throw out his activity all together?

We Question God's Hearing

Is God even listening to me? Does God even care?

The silence can be deafening at times. I grew up watching my parents pray. My mom would ask God for things; my dad would just thank God for things. My mom kept a prayer journal of what she asked. My dad just prayed for dinner. The older I get, the more I think I understand my father more. He grew up without a dad, spent time in a military school, his first wife left him—his only experience with God was his seeming silence. Where was God when all these things were going wrong? When he married again, had kids, and started going to church, he was still a bit skeptical if God hears any of us . . . especially him.

When you don't think God hears you, it's easy to just pray for dinner.

Many of us watched our parents pray and nothing happened. Then we prayed and nothing happened. Now when we pray, we just thank God for the food. At least that way, if he's not listening, nothing is at stake.

> When you don't think God hears you, it's easy to just pray for dinner.

Ever heard the phrase "hedging your bets"? It means to protect yourself from making the wrong choice. Like cheering for both teams in the Super Bowl. Or when a weather forecaster says, "The storm might hit land, or it might stay at sea." It takes the pressure off. I think I do this with God. It's much easier to ask God for a nice day or for travel mercies than it is to ask him to heal someone. I secretly wonder, *Is my faith strong enough that if God says no, I won't interpret it as he's not listening?* Haven't many of us wondered if we should just stop praying for an end to COVID-19?

We Question Our Part

I love the old movie *A Few Good Men*. It's a great movie investigating the death of a Marine that involves twists and turns and classic courtroom drama. There's a fantastic scene where the staunch, hardened Colonel Nathan Jessup (Jack Nicholson) is being questioned by Tom Cruise's character, Lieutenant Daniel Kaffee. Kaffee asks for some flight records from Jessup, at which Jessup is clearly annoyed. Finally, Jessup replies, "I will, on one condition." "What is that?" Kaffee asks. "You have to ask me nicely." Kaffee is confused by this seemingly elementary way of thinking. Then Jessup goes on a tirade about how he deserves some respect.

> Do our actions determine his answers?

I often think of that when I pray. I almost picture God saying, "You have to ask me nicely."

Is there a set of magic words we have to say in order to get God's attention? Do we need a certain number of *Hail Marys*, *Our Fathers*, and *Lord, I'm begging yous* to make him uncross his arms, lean forward, and give us what we want?

Do our actions determine his answers?

We Know a No Is Possible

In Joshua 7, we read of how one man's actions caused devastating results for an entire army. Israel was living under the blessing of God and on a tremendous winning streak when it came to battles and advancing their kingdom. But then, out of the blue, they suffered a surprising loss. Men were killed in battle and took off running from the people of Ai. Joshua went before God, asking for a reason why God backed out on his promise, and God quickly redirected Joshua to his own people. They were the ones who had broken the covenant.

After a morning inquiry, Achan, the son of Carmi from the tribe of Judah, finally confessed: "It is true! I have sinned against the LORD, the God of Israel. This is what I have done: When I saw in the plunder a beautiful robe from Babylonia, two hundred shekels of silver and a bar of gold weighing fifty shekels, I coveted them and took them" (Josh. 7:20–21). Because Achan had broken the covenant with God of not stealing from their conquests, he caused God to pull back his hand of blessing on their entire nation.

In the dark moments of God's silence in my life, this is what I wonder. Have I not upheld my end of the bargain? Have I violated God's law in some way? Is there some tiny clause from the fine print in Leviticus that I've overlooked? Am I Achan?

You may not have heard of Achan before, but you've probably wondered if you are like him. This is what we all fear. Did we do or not do something *before* we prayed that jeopardized our prayer? When disaster strikes my home, did I do something to cause it? When God seems silent, is it my fault? When a puppy isn't born, did I not pray enough? Is it my sister's fault for not praying at all? Our questions are all focused on our actions *before* we pray.

But what if there is another question to ask?

Can My Actions *after* My Prayer Determine His Answers?

Many options have been given to us regarding what to do before we pray.

Go into your room and be alone with God.

Stand in the church and cry out with other believers.

Confess your sins to God.

Confess your sins to your brothers and sisters in Christ.

Ask forgiveness from those you've wronged.

Take time to praise God for who he is and what he's done.

Sing at least one song by Chris Tomlin and one hymn.

THEN you may ask God for things. But did you ever wonder what to do *after* you pray?

Do my actions have anything to do with his answer?

Is there anything you and I might be doing, or not doing, that could cause us to not see God's answer? Or, perhaps worse, for God to choose to say no?

There are many moments in our lives when, regardless of past experiences and failures, we find ourselves so desperate that we cry out to God. We pour out our prayers, making promises, deals, and confessions, and then we say amen. And then we wait. And wait.

It feels like when you send a text to someone and pour out your heart . . . and then they start to text back. You see the three dots on the screen telling you they are responding, but it just takes forever. You keep checking. You refresh your screen. You even turn off the phone and turn it back on in case a signal was missed. And you still wait. For many of us, this describes our prayer life: staring at the three dots in the bubble.

When you look at the life and ministry of Jesus, you see that he has some very unique instructions for people not just *before* they pray, but also *after*. The ministry of Jesus shows us a variety of people who come to him in need. Some get an immediate answer, some have work to do, and some simply wait. But all these situations teach us what to do after we say amen. Think about the different responses people got after they made a request of Jesus:

> As much as the Scriptures have to say about what to do before we pray, Jesus gives us many examples of what to do after we pray.

"Get up, take up your mat, and go."

"Go and wash your eyes."

"Head home first."

"Go and show yourself to the priest."

"You figure it out."

"Stay here."

"Tell me, why should I?"

As much as the Scriptures have to say about what to do before we pray, Jesus gives us many examples of what to do after we pray.

Why would Jesus give such odd instructions? He's not one to waste words or efforts. Could it be that he's teaching us what to do while we wait on God? Could it be that the answer to our prayers hangs in the balance of what we do next? Could our understanding of God's action have everything to do with what we do after we say amen?

What Do We Do While We Wait for
God to Answer Our Prayers?

This is exactly the dilemma Mary faces early on in Jesus's adult life. He hasn't even started his public ministry yet. No one knows who he really is except Mary, Joseph, and John the Baptist. Any of his followers are simply thinking they are following a rabbi. When Jesus goes to a wedding, the unthinkable happens. They run out of wine! Whether or not you think wine should be consumed at a wedding or at all, they didn't have an issue with it back then. In fact, some scholars say that the lack of wine could result in a lawsuit. Back then, the wedding celebration didn't last a few hours after the ceremony with a dance floor and cutting the cake. The wedding party could last for days. After all, everyone had traveled so far, they might as well make the most of the celebration. And now they were out of wine.

Mary decides to bring her request to Jesus. This may be the first "prayer" to Jesus, and his reaction is stunning: "'Dear woman, that's not our problem,' Jesus replied. 'My time has not yet come'" (John 2:4 NLT).

There are some who think the reason she comes to Jesus is because as guests, they might have been responsible for bringing some wine. But either way, Jesus basically says no. But Mary believes he's about to do something: "But his mother told the servants, 'Do whatever he tells you'" (John 2:5 NLT).

We don't know if he winks at Mary. We don't know if he raises an eyebrow. The servants certainly don't know. They just know Mary says, "Do what he says." Even though the prayer has already been asked, even though it has already been denied, Jesus then tells them what to do next. "Standing nearby were six stone water jars, used for Jewish ceremonial washing. Each could hold twenty to thirty gallons. Jesus told the servants, 'Fill the jars with water'" (John 2:6–7 NLT).

Jesus tells the servants to fill these pots to the brim. All water, no wine—not even the residue of wine. Aside from meeting the needs of the wedding, this miracle would make a very nice wedding gift.

Think about how heavy these would be. They would weigh roughly three hundred pounds apiece when filled. Walk a jar down to the river, fill it up, bring it back. Now, do it five more times. In the heat. While dressed for a wedding. And every time, they think, *Why are we doing this?*

> When the jars had been filled, he said, "Now dip some out, and take it to the master of ceremonies." So the servants followed his instructions.
>
> When the master of ceremonies tasted the water that was now wine, not knowing where it had come from (though, of course, the servants knew), he called the bridegroom over. "A host always serves the best wine first," he said. "Then, when everyone has had a lot to drink, he brings out the less expensive wine. But you have kept the best until now!"
>
> This miraculous sign at Cana in Galilee was the first time Jesus revealed his glory. And his disciples believed in him. (John 2:7–11 NLT)

I think the key phrase here is "When the jars had been filled." Not when the request was made. Not when the first jar was brought back filled. Not after the third jar did they begin to smell the bouquet of wine, but only after all the jars had been filled. After they had done everything Jesus told them to do, then the miracle was made known.

God is faithful not just while we wait, but while we work. And our actions after the prayer can determine his answer.

In her book *Unglued*, Lysa TerKeurst says:

> Ultimately, the responsibility for winning this battle we're facing doesn't belong to us. We're not responsible for figuring it all out. Our job is simply to be obedient to God in the midst of what we're facing. God's job is results. Obedience positions us in the flow of God's power, working with God's ways instead of against God's ways. Are you overwhelmed with money issues? Look up verses on money and start applying God's Word to your bank account and your bills. . . . Having marital problems? Look up biblical truths addressed to husbands and wives and start applying them. . . . Dealing with friendship troubles? Same thing.

So let me ask you: What's the prayer you've prayed that has you waiting on God? Is it a prayer for healing? Is it a prayer for relational reconciliation? Is it a prayer for peace in your spirit? Is it a prayer for hope in your family? Is it a prayer for transformation in your spouse? And do you feel like you are looking at three blinking dots in a bubble while you wait for God to respond?

Could he be waiting on you to fill some jars? Could it be that you are only on your first trip out of six to the river? Maybe the answer you seek is found while you work, while you wait.

So, what should you be doing *after* you say amen?

Discussion Questions

1. What steps do you take *before* you pray?

2. What assumptions do you make when God is silent?

3. What is a prayer you are currently praying and for which you have yet to hear an answer from God?

4. What is a prayer you have given up praying?

5. How do you think God speaks to us?

Next Steps

1. Take time to write your prayer requests down, either in a journal, an app on your phone, or a whiteboard at home.

2. Ask others for their prayer requests so that you have an equal mix of requests for you and requests for others.

Was It Something
I Said?

I was headed to Atlanta to meet up with some pastor friends, and we were trying to plan out our three days. There were churches to visit, places to see, and, of course, local restaurants to try. Atlanta is filled with amazing food and exciting places, and I thought, *Why waste an opportunity?* I pulled out my Food Network App and searched "Diners, Drive-Ins and Dives" locations in Atlanta. Surprisingly, I had already visited all of those (apparently, I've been to Atlanta a few times). Then I thought, *Why check an app when you can ask a local?*

I texted a friend of mine who was an Atlantean and well-versed in Atlanta cuisine. I said, "Where should we go?" He said, "How adventurous are you?" I replied, "We are three pastors in a big city—what do you think?" He replied in what seemed like a whispered tone, almost as if he was being watched: "There's a great place that requires a secret passcode. You go into an old-time phone booth outside a seemingly abandoned building, and you dial a secret number on the phone, and the wall will open up. Trust me. This message will self-destruct in 30 seconds." (Okay, maybe I added that last part.) He went on to give me the number, and I told my friends, "Well, this is either going to be an epic evening or an epic fail. Either way, it will be memorable."

We drove around the city block searching for the address until finally we saw this building that looked to be all dark and abandoned. Sure enough, there was a phone booth. I crept into the phone booth quietly and bravely picked up the phone and dialed the number. I waited for what seemed to be an eternity . . . and finally, the wall that the phone was on swung open to a packed restaurant. The music was pumping, the people were talking and laughing, and the scent of food was enticing. He was right. This would be an event that we would never forget.

When we left, we had to exit the phone booth again. We saw random people scattered around waiting to get in. They'd heard the legend of this place, but they didn't have the number. Slowly, people began to saunter up to us and ask, "How'd you get in?" "What's it like?" "Can I have the number?"

I was faced with a dilemma. What would you do? (Let's just say, I would not do well as an undercover spy being interrogated.)

This is exactly the way I feel about prayer—like it's a closed-door party I can't enter. Almost like the Father, the Son, and the Holy Spirit are hosting a wonderful evening of conversation and granting prayer requests, but the only ones who are able to enjoy it are the ones who have the secret passcode. Maybe it's sincerity, maybe it's the right combination of words, maybe it's who you know, but it seems obvious to me that there are some who are in and some who feel left out.

Every week, I greet people after service and I listen to them tell me their troubles: "I'm losing my kids in a custody battle," or, "The doctor said it's cancer," or, "My husband wants a divorce." And I say, "Have you prayed about it?" And they say, "Yes. But it didn't do any good," or, "It didn't work for me," or "Nothing changed." What they are saying is: "How do you get in to the prayer-request-granting party?"

Even though I'm a pastor and I teach people how to pray, the truth is I still struggle with prayer. I often wonder if I pray enough, if I am praying the right way, or if I am even getting through to God. In fact, one of the reasons I'm writing this book is that I'd like to debunk a lot of the myths that I believe about prayer and the fears I have about unanswered prayer. Because, at the end of the day, I have the same questions you do: "How'd you get in?" "What's it like?" "Can I have the number?"

> "How do you get in to the prayer-request-granting party?"

Coming to Prayer in Faith

My lack of connection at times is not for a lack of promised access. Jesus made a lot of promises about prayer. Take a look at these words he says to his disciples in the upper room the night before he was crucified:

> I tell you the truth, anyone who believes in me will
> do the same works I have done, and even greater

works, because I am going to be with the Father. You
can ask for anything in my name, and I will do it,
so that the Son can bring glory to the Father. Yes,
ask me for anything in my name, and I will do it!
(John 14:12–14 NLT)

But if you remain in me and my words remain in you,
you may ask for anything you want, and it will be
granted! (John 15:7 NLT)

You didn't choose me. I chose you. I appointed you to
go and produce lasting fruit, so that the Father will
give you whatever you ask for, using my name.
(John 15:16 NLT)

At that time you won't need to ask me for anything. I
tell you the truth, you will ask the Father directly, and
he will grant your request because you use my name.
You haven't done this before. Ask, using my name,
and you will receive, and you will have abundant joy.
(John 16:23–24 NLT)

Well, yes, you may be thinking. *But, that was to the disciples.
Maybe that's not for me.*

Okay, let's expand the audience. These next two passages
from Jesus are from his teachings to multitudes of people, not
just the chosen few:

Keep on asking, and you will receive what you ask for.
Keep on seeking, and you will find. Keep on knocking, and the door will be opened to you. For everyone
who asks, receives. Everyone who seeks, finds. And

to everyone who knocks, the door will be opened.
(Matt. 7:7–8 NLT)

I also tell you this: If two of you agree here on earth
concerning anything you ask, my Father in heaven
will do it for you. (Matt. 18:19 NLT)

Don't these promises sound amazing? Ask and it will be
given. Seek and you will find. Knock and the door will be
opened. Agree and it shall be done. I'd love to have this evident
in my life.

I was helping lead a youth retreat for our church years ago
when we attended a national conference. We took hundreds
of kids on charter buses, and on the way home, we decided to
stop at McDonald's for lunch. I saw the line of kids and thought,
I don't want to wait. So I walked up to a young man named
Ryan and said, "Here's $20. Will you get me a number 5? And
keep the change for your lunch." He looked at me a bit stunned,
but said "Sure. Thanks." I went and sat down, feeling incredi-
bly righteous for my generosity. Later, I learned that Ryan had
given all his money the night before during the offering time,
and he believed God would provide for his lunch on the way
home. And then to top it off, he actually got in line with no
money in his pocket! Suddenly, my feelings of righteous generosity paled in comparison to his astounding faith.

I don't know about you, but if I'm being completely honest,
I don't see evidence of that type of faith in my life. Do you?
I can't imagine just getting in line with no money, believing
something will happen.

In legendary stories of prayer warriors and missionaries,
we see people who are proactively waiting. They pray, and then

they move ahead expecting their request to be granted. Many of us, myself included, pray . . . then take a more hesitant posture in waiting.

Here are a few common options:

- Lighting a candle or incense
- Telling someone else after-the-fact about the prayer
- Praying at a later time for the same purpose
- Worrying—whether about the situation or about praying with the proper attitude
- Journaling
- Reading Scripture or other Christian writings

It's almost a posture of crossing my fingers and hoping for the best. It's much less than getting in line hoping for God to come through. My tendency is to start scrolling through potential reasons why God is silent, rather than to have an optimistic expectation that he's about to speak.

And once God is silent for more than five minutes, I begin to come up with my "reasons why this didn't work" list, complete with a "how to fix this for the next time" manual.

Here's my checklist of what I wonder.

Did I Talk Too Much?

Jesus says in his famous Sermon on the Mount that we shouldn't go on babbling like the Pharisees, for our Father knows what we need before we ask. *So, maybe,* I wonder, *I'm just bothering him.* Sometimes my youngest daughter will come to me with a request and it comes with a great amount of pleading: "Please can we . . . please can we . . . please can we . . ." And something in me says, *Well, not now! Stop it! Enough already!* Jesus goes on to say, "Don't think you will be heard because of your many words."

I know when I pray out of desperation—pleading, begging, pacing, and kneeling—and sense silence after all that, I begin to think, *That's it. I must have worn out my welcome.*

Is this something you wonder about? Perhaps I asked too much. Perhaps I asked too often. I want him to know I'm still interested, but I don't want to be a pest. Is God like us in that manner? Is he a parent that we think can be worn down, or more like a temperamental teacher who just wants to get back to teaching the class and we keep asking if we can go to the bathroom?

Did I Not Ask Enough?
On the other hand, Jesus tells the story of a friend who has a visitor at midnight. The friend goes next door and asks to borrow some bread to feed his guests. The neighbor says, "Go away," but the friend keeps knocking on the door. Jesus says, "Will he not finally get out of bed and give his friend food because of his persistence?" This is the equivalent of Jesus saying that if you pray enough, you might finally twist God's arm to the point he'll say, "Enough already! Here's your bread; just go away!" Is that what he's saying? If that's the case, maybe I haven't asked enough.

Many times, I've prayed for months about something just fearing that maybe I was one more ask away from God saying, okay. I didn't want to quit too early. I've read the stories of faithful people and churches who make their demands of God like they are trying to "Occupy heaven," and after days or weeks or months, they finally get their yes. Makes me wonder how many of these stories received a no, and it was never reported on social media like the yes was!

Is this a tendency for you? To worry that your prayers are just a few repetitions away from cracking the code? Like this is a Harry Potter type of spell and I just need to get the words and actions down and performed in the right way and the right amount of times and it will work. Do I need a magic wand?

Did I Not Have Enough Faith?

In the Gospels, there's a very strange story in which Jesus takes issue with a fig tree. Walking by it, he curses it and says, "May you never bear fruit again." The disciples are a bit stunned by this miracle:

> Then Jesus told them, "I tell you the truth, if you have faith and don't doubt, you can do things like this and much more. You can even say to this mountain, 'May you be lifted up and thrown into the sea,' and it will happen. You can pray for anything, and if you have faith, you will receive it." (Matt. 21:21–22 NLT)

That sounds rather promising! Most of the time, I don't even need for a mountain to throw itself into the sea. I'd just like to see someone healed, someone get out of jail, or someone's marriage survive. So, when it doesn't happen, is that because I didn't have enough faith?

I'm embarrassed to say how much weight I've carried over my lifetime thinking that my lack of faith was the reason someone didn't get a yes from God. On more than one occasion, I've stood beside someone on their deathbed and prayed, "Lord, we pray for healing, but if you choose to take them, may they go in peace and may you be glorified and we be comforted," only to have a family member take me out into the hall and chastise me for my lack of faith. "Pastor, don't pray for a peaceful passing; pray for healing! If you'd have more faith, they would live."

Have you lived with that weight? If only you had had more faith, your parents wouldn't have divorced. Or your mother would have lived. Or your son wouldn't have overdosed. It's a terrible burden to carry. But is it necessary?

What if you had faith in the wrong thing? In other words, did my prayer of faith that God would take them home cause God to take them home rather than heal them?

My friend Brenda told me about a burden she carried as a child for years. Her family had all boys with the exception of her. When she learned her mom was pregnant, Brenda began praying for a girl. But when her mom miscarried, and it was discovered the baby would have been another boy, Brenda feared her prayer had caused this miscarriage. As adults, we look at this and say, "Oh, of course not." But don't we also create and carry our own unnecessary burdens? It's almost like we are fearful that God is the genie in the lamp who will do exactly as we say—so choose your words carefully!

Did I pray for my kids to get into the *wrong* college on accident?

Did I pray for my father to rest in peace when he could have lived?

Did I pray for this job and now I regret it?

Is God easily manipulated or tricked by our faith—or lack thereof?

Did I Not Have Enough Passion?

One day, Jesus is sitting at a well in Samaria and a woman comes out to draw water. This situation was so scandalous in its time; I can imagine it is the kind of story that would make TMZ ecstatic. After all, you have a gender tension: a man talking to a woman; you have an ethnic tension: a Jew talking to a Samaritan; and you have religious tension: a rabbi talking to a sinner. Yet despite all the cultural reasons Jesus *shouldn't* share insight into prayer with this woman, it is during their conversation about faith and religion that Jesus drops a truth bomb on her that shakes my prayer life every time I sense distance from God: "the true worshipers will worship the Father in the Spirit and in truth" (John 4:23).

Now, I recognize that the capital "S" in Spirit is letting us know this is the Holy Spirit, but since I often interpret Scripture through the lens of, How does this apply to me *right now*? I can read the word "Spirit" as "spirited" or passion. In other words, I hear Jesus saying: The true worshippers will worship God with lots of spirit and truth. This sends me down a list of "maybes":

- Maybe I need to cry more.
- Maybe I need to beg more.
- Maybe I need to sing first, stand for hours, kneel all night.
- Maybe I need to bring more textual proof to God.
- Maybe I need to remind him how he's done this for others; now it's my turn.
- Maybe I need to have others pray and testify that I deserve it.

I'm not saying my thinking is accurate or even logical; but in my darkest hour of need, it seems the most rational.

So, is that it? I just needed more passion to prove my point? Do you live with that pain?

For all of us reserved in spirit and introverted in nature, praying with passion is like trying to write with our left hand, if we're right-handed. It feels forced; it's not natural. But is that what it takes? Do I need to raise my hands in worship? Do I need to speak in tongues? David danced before God in his underwear. And when asked about it, he said, "I'll become even more undignified than this!" Is that what I need to do? What if I run through the mall on Black Friday in my underwear? It might get me arrested; but if it works, don't the ends justify the means?

Answered Prayers—Just Not Mine

So, what is the problem? Why does God respond to some, but not others?

Even Habakkuk, one of God's prophets, wondered this. His pleading with God is chronicled in the Bible in the book bearing his name. Dianna Hobbs sums it up in her blog post "God Is Your Defense, Deliverer, and Helper": "Although he was anointed and powerfully used by God, he complained that the Lord was taking too long to answer him. 'How long, LORD, must I call for help, but you do not listen?'" [Hab. 1:2].

> Why does God respond to some, but not others?

Sociologists Dr. Daniel Winchester and Dr. Jeff Guhin noticed how many of us often fret about whether or not our prayers have been "performed" with enough sincerity or with the right attitude or disposition. In their work *Praying Straight from the Heart*, they note that most of us start worrying about our sincerity in the prayer the moment we say amen. In other words, all of our waiting on God has led us further from God rather than closer to God.

Since we are friends now and I'm sharing my soul, can I tell you one of the stories that really bugs me in regard to God's silence in my life?

The Gospel of Mark tells us that one day, Jesus encountered a man who had been possessed by a host of demons. And even though they are demons, they have a request of Jesus:

> Then the evil spirits begged him again and again not to send them to some distant place. There happened to be a large herd of pigs feeding on the hillside nearby. "Send us into those pigs," the spirits begged. "Let us enter them." (Mark 5:10–12 NLT)

What's shocking to me is not their begging for mercy; it's Jesus's answer:

> So Jesus gave them permission. The evil spirits came out of the man and entered the pigs, and the entire herd of about 2,000 pigs plunged down the steep hillside into the lake and drowned in the water. (v. 13 NLT)

Are you serious?

I pray for kids dying of cancer, marriages on the brink of divorce, drug-addicted teens, the end of human trafficking, wildfires to be put out, school shootings to cease, COVID-19 victims to be healed, and I feel at times like I'm not getting a cell signal to heaven. And then demons make a request, and they get an immediate, "Sure!"

Does anybody else feel this way?

Maybe it's my lack of passion, lack of faith—talking too much, yet not enough.

Maybe the problem is just . . . me.

Discussion Questions

1. When you pray, how soon do you expect an answer?

2. What do you tend to assume when God seems silent?

3. Who do you tend to blame?

4. What do you do when you have been waiting a long time?

5. Much like the demons getting their wish, do you have any examples of answered prayers that bother you?

Next Steps

1. Make a list of what you tend to think when God is silent.

2. Share this list with a friend.

What Do I Do Now?

I took four years of guitar lessons when I was a kid, so that basically makes me an expert . . . Well, not really, but it made me think so. Years later, I still knew enough to play the chords G, C, and D, which allowed me to play the beginning of "Free Falling" and most worship songs, so that was all I needed. Years later in college, I had a friend who had a guitar that seemed out of tune. Even though I was years removed from my guitar lessons, I just knew that I could tune it.

I started working on that guitar like I had built it. Tuning, turning the strings, and yet . . . still not right. I took it down to the lobby where there was a piano (yes, I went to a Christian college; pianos in the lobby were standard issue in case a sing-spiration broke out). I began tuning against the piano, and still, it was not right. Suddenly, it had reached its limit. With one more turn of the peg, I had tuned too far . . . and the string broke. It's a startling sound and can also cause an injury if a broken guitar string snaps back against your skin. And it did. I looked at my friend who was a bit stunned and said, "Hmm, guess I couldn't tune it."

Now, there were several problems that day: an old guitar, my inexperience, and, mainly, my arrogance. But another problem, unknown to me at the time, was that the piano was out of tune. Even if I knew what I was doing but was still tuning against this piano, it would have never been tuned correctly.

Years later, I learned an interesting fact about piano tuning. (Yes, I know you can tune a piano, but you can't tuna fish.) If you tune a piano with a tuning fork, you can't use that piano to tune another piano. In fact, if you did that repeatedly from piano to piano, though the lack of precision seems minuscule, over time, you would be way out of tune. You can only tune against the pure source: the tuning fork.

Now, you might be asking, Why the music lesson? Because when we "tune" our view of God from pastors, churches, books, parents, friends, or even preferences, we may be close, but we are not precise. And over time, we define God *our* way, not *the* way.

Then, if we aren't careful, we take our imperfect view of God and run Jesus through that filter. If we think God is vengeful and angry, we'll read every word of Jesus as condemning and a bit snarky. If we think God is passive and not interested, we'll see Jesus as biding time until he can get back to heaven. In fact, many of us have what I call *The Fly* version of God and Jesus.

Remember the old movie *The Fly*? Some may remember the original black-and-white film with Vincent Price. I remember the one from the eighties with Jeff Goldblum (I had to sneak into it as a kid). It was the story of a scientist who thought he had developed a machine that could teleport people from one location to another. He gave it a try by climbing into the chamber; but unbeknownst to him, a tiny housefly had landed in there as well. Their DNA was combined, and while he appeared to be fine, over the course of the movie, he became a six-foot-tall insect. A bit far-fetched, but still an accurate representation of what we do to God. In our naivety and wishful thinking, we end up creating a monster.

My tendency is to define God based off the wrong thing.

How Others Represent God

The world is filled with "ustas" (*yu-stas*). I "usta" be a Christian. I "usta" go to church. I "usta" pray. Ask a few questions and you begin to hear that their story of what led them away from God really had nothing to do with God, but rather their disappointment with someone who represented God.

We've all heard and experienced our fair share of horror stories from abusive church leaders and televangelists. Often, our bad experiences are the result of well-meaning people who were tripped up by their own humanity. Judgmentalism, hypocrisy, and even good old-fashioned arrogance got in the way of their trying to live out the Christian life. But should that define God?

One of the greatest composers in history was Johann Sebastian Bach. From "Ave Maria" to "Air on a G String," most of us have heard his amazing work. Even if you are not a fan of classical music, you most likely can appreciate some of these timeless masterpieces. But let's say a junior high band decided to tackle one of these. They worked for weeks on the piece and then presented it at the town Christmas performance. Even though all the parents would find it charming, most of us would find it a disaster. That being said, would it be accurate to judge Bach and all classical music on this one performance? Of course not; these musicians are novices at best.

Yet, most of us adapt our view of God from others trying to "perform" his best works of forgiveness, love, and acceptance. When it comes to my prayer life, I have to remember how God answers me is not always clearly seen in how *others* represent him.

How I Would Be "God"

Another improper "tuning fork" for how I see God is in what I would do if I were God. In the sports world, we refer to this as "Armchair Quarterback"—the idea that it's easy to make decisions from my La-Z-Boy chair in my living room as opposed to on the field in real time.

Not sure about you, but my mind can often drift to, *If I were God, I would . . .* Here are just a few of my thoughts:

- End human trafficking
- Cure cancer
- Wipe out all mosquitoes

Not saying these are all of equal value; just part of my list.

I like what Andy Stanley often says in his messages: "If we could see as God sees, we'd be more likely to do as God says." Seeing from his vantage point is everything. And yet, there's no way we can fully do that. It's like trying to explain air to a fish. They live underwater; they don't even have the capacity to understand. Those of us who are stuck in time and the finiteness of life have a governor on our understanding. It's impossible for me to impose my preferences on a God who knows all and sees all.

How to See God

Philip felt the same way we do. After three years of walking with Jesus and listening to him talk about God, he finally caves and says, "Just show us the Father." You can almost hear his exasperation. "You've talked *about* the Father; you've talked *to* the Father; you are now saying you are *going* to the Father. Would you pull back the veil? We'd like to see the wizard; we'd like to see for ourselves. Would you show us the Father?" To which Jesus says words that would change history: "Anyone who has seen me has seen the Father" (John 14:9).

In other words, the only way to properly see God is to look through the lens of Jesus. The only way to see the Father is through the Son. He is the true "tuning fork" for all. Since that is the case, let's take some time to walk through how Jesus answered requests.

I Thought You'd Never Ask

Sometimes it's as if he's just waiting on us. We see Jesus do this when a woman reaches out to him to heal her from what the Scriptures refer to as "an issue of blood." It's a crowded street. There is a mob of people swarming around Jesus, and she just sneaks up without saying a word. She doesn't even ask; she just reaches out and touches him, having faith that this would be enough to help her. It turns out it was just what was needed. Jesus stops traffic and turns to find her, commending her faith and verifying her healing.

There are times I've been at my wits' end with problem solving, and finally I stop and pray. It's almost as if I can sense God saying, "It's about time." Sometimes the problem is resolved; but often, the peace that comes over me is overwhelming. Out of the peace comes clarity—which breeds solutions. I wonder how long I missed out because I hadn't asked yet?

Yes, and Here's More!

I'm always struck by the small detail in the miracle of the feeding of the five thousand. Jesus is handed a sack lunch that the disciples seemingly stole from a kid (thus originating the age-old bullying phrase "give me your lunch money"), and then he turns it into enough to feed five thousand people. This is what gets the headlines. Jesus feeds five thousand people! Which probably was more like fifteen thousand, since they usually only counted the men. But the detail missed in the fine print is the phrase, "And the disciples picked up twelve basketfuls of broken pieces that were left over" (Matt. 14:20). All kinds of symbolism are here in regard to the twelve disciples and the twelve tribes of Israel; but the main point is that sometimes with Jesus, our requests turn into a yes—with leftovers!

A few times in our church's history, I remember praying for a few baptisms only to see hundreds. I always walk away humbled by my lack of faith and God's view of extravagance. Other times, I've prayed for God to send just a couple of volunteers to help us with a project, only to watch dozens show up. It's as if God says, "Yes, and here's more!" God seems to know what the task requires.

Yes, But Not the Way You Thought

Because Jesus sees things from a different perspective, he knows our greatest need, even if we don't. When a group of men bring their paralyzed friend to Jesus, they are hoping for Jesus to heal his physical ailment. They climb up on the roof of the room in which Jesus is teaching, tear off the shingles, and begin to lower their friend down into the crowded room like he is Ethan Hunt in *Mission: Impossible*. Jesus takes one look at him and says, "Your sins are forgiven" (Luke 5:20). Now, that's not what he came for, but Jesus knew that the bigger issue in this man's life was with his soul, not his body. That being said, he then goes on to help him walk again. But certainly, this was not exactly how these men thought this day would go.

Another time, Jesus walks by a paraplegic who day in and day out would rest by the pool of Bethesda, a place that was thought to have healing powers. Jesus asks one question: "Do you want to get well?" (John 5:6). The man's reply implies he has no idea who Jesus is. His request is for someone to help him into the healing pool. Jesus meets his needs, but in a different way . . . he tells him to get up and walk.

Have you ever had those moments? I've prayed for my kids to have friends at school, only to see them be a friend to those in need. Not what I prayed for—probably should have been—but God had another idea. My mom used to pray for God to make ends meet; and he did, but not through an anonymous check in the mail, but rather through my dad being able to always fix our cars. After years of this, my dad started saying, "The Lord will provide."

Not at This Time

Sometimes Jesus's response is a matter of timing. As mentioned in the first chapter, Jesus's own mother wanted him to save the day at a wedding, to which he replied, "It's not time yet" . . . and then goes ahead and does it. I've always wondered about that. Was "the right time" fifteen minutes away? Did Jesus just change his mind? Either that, or, clearly, Jesus has his own timetable.

Another time, the masses cry out to him: "Just show us a sign." Jesus says no—partly because he knows their wicked hearts and partly because the sign they need is to see the resurrection. This will come in time.

I came across an interesting perspective from author and speaker Beth Moore. She asks, What if God withholds our desires from us because he knows what those desires might cost us? Perhaps we can have faith that a greater yes is in process while we live with the no for now.

We've seen this in our own church. We prayed for land and a building for years. Every time we'd get close, the city would shut us down. I found myself getting so frustrated with God. After all, we were trying to do a good thing! Years later, after we saw God say yes to this prayer, it was clear that he had been protecting us from smaller dreams. When he finally said yes, it was obvious that for years he had been saying, "Right idea, just not the right time." (More to come on that one.)

No, Because I Love You Too Much

While Jesus is on the cross, the mockers cry out to him, "If you are God, then come down off that cross." Of course, they are sarcastic in their claims, but Jesus knows that he could come down and make their jaws drop. He'd save his "dignity," but they'd lose their souls. In this case, in his compassion for the world, his answer is "No, because I love you too much."

And perhaps the greatest example of this is the answer Jesus receives from the Father in the garden. "Will you take this cup from me?" And the answer is "No, because I love you—and *them*—too much."

While reading through a collection of writings in the book *Devotional Classics*, I was challenged by Martin Luther telling us to pray by "fixing our mind on some pressing need and desiring it with all earnestness." And then not long after that, I read from St. Bernard (the man, not the dog—maybe that's only funny to me) that we should never doubt in our prayers because God is always working for our good. Either our prayer will be granted, or we will be protected from its granting.

And if words from Martin Luther and St. Bernard aren't enough, can I quote Garth Brooks? "Some of God's greatest gifts are unanswered prayers." Mic drop.

Understanding the five ways that God answers prayers is helpful, but it still leaves us with our initial problem: What do we do while we wait for God's answer to be revealed?

I think I speak for most of us when I say one of my least favorite things to do is to wait. And the place I find this to be the most frustrating is at the doctor's office. I make the appointment,

I show up on time, and yet, I still have to wait. Why is that? Sometimes they give me things to do: fill out these forms, pay this copay, update your insurance. Sometimes they move me from one room to the next, performing minor tests of weight, blood pressure, and the like. And sometimes they say nothing. I sit in a room with other impatient people who are all trying to not be worried about what the doctor may say and trying not to be too anxious for the doctor to fix them. We sort through old magazines, watch game shows on TV, and mindlessly scroll through our phones. We make small talk, we stare at our shoes, and we hope that we will be the next person called.

Waiting on God can feel similar. We gather in churches and Bible studies, and we pray for a quick resolve. We try to distract and numb ourselves with technology and even medications. We busy ourselves with life and try to act like we aren't nervous or frustrated. We walk the tightrope of faith and doubt and wonder where God is. We celebrate with others when they get their answer from God; but inside, we wonder, *Why not us?* And slowly, after enough silence, we stop wondering about God, and we begin to wander from God.

> After enough silence, we stop wondering about God, and we begin to wander from God.

In my moments in the doctor's waiting room, I have to remember the words of the receptionist: "Listen carefully for your name to be called." I'm reminded how easily I can get distracted. I listen to the couple next to me arguing about how often he takes his medication. I listen to *Family Feud* on the TV. I listen to a podcast on my phone. And before long, I've distracted myself with the room and forgotten to listen for my name.

Adam McHugh reminds us in his work *The Listening Life* that the foundation of our faith is listening: "The centerpiece of Israel's prayer life, the Shema, begins with the word *hear.*" He believes that God gives listening to people as a tool to connect with him: "[Listening] is a gift from God to us that sparks intimacy . . . and that assures us of guidance and the awareness of God's presence." McHugh notes that many Christians focus primarily on listening to the Bible in order to experience the words of God. He pushes against this claim and says, "I am concerned that restricting God's self-communication to words written on papyrus thousands of years ago opens our faith to becoming as dusty as some of our study Bibles." Furthermore, McHugh says, "I am convinced that a listening, conversational relationship with God is supposed to be the most natural thing in the world."

I wish this were more natural for me.

Ghosted by God

Specifically after moments of listening to God through the Scriptures, McHugh says that people should act on what they have heard. He names this action "improvisation" and pushes back against the idea that people should only hear and not act. In the words of McHugh, "Our improvisation flows from what we have heard, and with the Scriptures ringing in our ears, we move forward to create something new and stirring, a piece that is compelling to those who listen to us."

He explains that many people do not experience communication with God, and writes, "For many people, the idea that the world, the church, or they themselves have been ghosted by God is deeply resonant." I can connect with that. I've felt the sting of being blocked on social media from someone, or unfriended, or even ghosted on a text message. It is like I've been told, "I'm no longer listening to you."

But despite all my fears of God ghosting me, the life of Jesus reminds me that he's always pursuing me. The very fact that Jesus showed up is "good news for all," as the angels declared. God has come near. He is moving, acting, listening, and speaking.

So maybe the issue isn't so much him, or even his answers, but rather how I listen.

Over the remainder of this book, we are going to listen. And then respond. Active waiting, as some might say.

We will walk through seven steps Jesus gives us to follow while we wait. Some of these will speed up God's process, some will settle our minds, and some will change our hearts. But all will help us hear from God. And all of them help those of us who feel stuck in God's waiting room longing to hear him call our name.

At the end of each chapter is a collection of prayers that can be prayed while you sit in your waiting room. Pray them daily, pray them with others, and pray them with honesty.

Listen carefully for your name to be called.

Discussion Questions

1. What waiting room do you find you sit in the most?

2. What is the most common answer you have heard from God?

3. How long does it normally take for you to recognize an answer from God?

4. What surprises you about the way Jesus answers requests?

5. If you could ask God one question, and get a verbal answer, what would it be?

Next Steps

1. Start keeping a prayer journal of your requests.

2. Start filling in these requests with one of the five answers God gives.

4

Align with the "Why"

My youngest daughter has figured out the secret to asking her parents for things. It's a skill all kids learn at some point. And she has perfected it. It's one thing to go to your parents and ask, "Can I have ice cream for dinner?" or "Can we go to Disneyland tomorrow?" Those are pretty easy.

But when she says, "Dad, can I download this new social media app so I can better communicate with you during the day?" or "Can I stay home from school today so we can spend some quality time together?" it's a little trickier.

Why is that? Because she's appealing to my "why."

As parents, our "why"—meaning our purpose or goal in parenting—is to create great relationships with our kids so they'll want to return when they leave.

And when she asks about ice cream or Disney, while it might help to accomplish some of that, it's a bit of a stretch. But when she can take something she wants—an app or ditching school—and couple it with my "why"... well, then she knows that is something that makes me pause and think.

You have a "why" in parenting. Maybe it's to raise well-behaved kids or help them get into a great college or have a better childhood than you had. Whatever it is, I bet your kids have figured it out, and at least one of them has discovered a way to leverage that to get what they want.

While God is not a parent to be manipulated, he is still a parent. The first thing Jesus tells us to call him is "Father." This is more than our "Lord" or "boss" or "King"—all of which are noteworthy and accurate. But Jesus asks us to call him "Father." Lean into the relational angle of your connection. If God truly is our Father, it will benefit us to understand his "why."

Recently, while undergoing a season of emptiness in my prayer time, I began to wonder: *Why can't my prayers seem to get past the ceiling? Why do I continue to hear silence when I speak? Why do I feel like I need to muster up energy and emotion to get his attention? Do I need sackcloth and ashes? Do I need to fast more ... or from different things? Maybe my celery fast wasn't enough.* (Kidding, sort of). Maybe the bigger issue is that my prayers aren't aligned with his "why."

We see Jesus has marching orders different than we might presume. Early in his ministry, while it might appear he is traveling about building a name for himself with healings left and right, Matthew reminds us there was a purpose behind it: "That evening many demon-possessed people were brought to Jesus. He cast out the evil spirits with a simple command, and he healed all the sick. This fulfilled the word of the Lord through the prophet Isaiah, who said, 'He took our sicknesses and removed our diseases'" (Matt. 8:16–17 NLT).

The Wrong "Why"

I love the event that takes place with Jesus and his three closest friends: Peter, James, and John. Jesus gives these guys a front row seat to his glory. They trudge up a hill, and Jesus is suddenly accompanied by Elijah and Moses. What an amazing moment this must have been for these three Jewish boys. They would have only heard stories about these two faith legends—at best had their trading cards in their bike spokes. So, with that in mind, Peter's reaction is to figure out a way to make the magic last. He shouts out, "We should build three shelters—one for each!" He's thinking like a kid on the last day of summer camp: "How can we all stay together forever?" However, Matthew tells us in his Gospel, "But even as he spoke, a bright cloud overshadowed them, and a voice from the cloud said, 'This is my dearly loved Son, who brings me great joy. Listen to him'" (Matt. 17:5 NLT).

In other words, God the Father interrupted what Peter was saying because it was too ridiculous to continue. I'm sure John was the one who told the rest of the guys, "Right in the middle of Peter's stupid idea, God the Father cut him off!" (Matt. 17 RUSTY GEORGE VERSION).

In other words, this is not God's "why." In that moment, God communicates to Peter and the disciples: "This idea is short term . . . I'm thinking long term. Your idea is earthly . . . I'm thinking eternal."

Another time, Jesus is visiting his friends Mary, Martha, and Lazarus. This had to be a very exciting time—not just for them, but also for Jesus. They were all very close. It was a great time for Jesus to relax among close friends and a great time for this family to enjoy Jesus. But when the pastor arrives, the potluck begins. Martha is busy in the kitchen preparing the fried chicken and potato salad, and Mary is in the family room listening to Jesus tell stories. Martha is a bit perturbed. I can appreciate this. I sometimes feel a gravitational pull toward working for Jesus more than being with Jesus. So she storms into the living room and tattles on Mary: "Jesus, don't you think she should help? After all, I'm being a servant! I seem to recall that being big on your list." Jesus surprises Mary and even the rest of us when he says, "She's focused on the right thing." In other words, "Serving me is not my 'why.' Being with me is."

Not long after this, Jesus starts fielding some requests from others. One man says to him, "Tell my brother to give me my share of the inheritance!" In those days, the older son got two-thirds, and the younger got one-third. This guy decides to take up the issue with Jesus, most likely in the presence of his brother: "Make him give me half instead of one-third!" he demands. Jesus's response is priceless: "Friend, who made me a judge over you to decide such things as that?" (Luke 12:14 NLT). Not Jesus's "why."

> "Serving me is not my 'why.' Being with me is."

You would think the disciples would figure out his "why" by this point. But not so fast. At what must have been a rather awkward dinner moment, the mother of James and John approaches Jesus, seemingly in front of everyone I might add, and says, "Would you make sure my boys get to sit on your right and left in your kingdom?" Jesus says, "Not for me to decide." In other words, Jesus is saying, "You got the kingdom part right, but wrong type of kingdom. Not earthly, but eternal. Not my 'why.'"

Another James, the half-brother of Jesus, wrote this in regard to God's "why":

> If you need wisdom, ask our generous God, and he will give it to you. He will not rebuke you for asking. But when you ask him, be sure that your faith is in God alone. Do not waver, for a person with divided loyalty is as unsettled as a wave of the sea that is blown and tossed by the wind. Such people should not expect to receive anything from the Lord. Their loyalty is divided between God and the world, and they are unstable in everything they do. (James 1:5–8 NLT)

Did you catch that? "Divided between God and the world." We tend to focus on the amount of faith; James reminds us that it's all about the direction of our faith and if we have the "why" of God in mind.

"And we are confident that he hears us whenever we ask for anything that pleases him. And since we know he hears us when we make our requests, we also know that he will give us what we ask for" (1 John 5:14–15 NLT).

There it is again: "anything that pleases him." Not always what pleases us, but him. His "why"; not mine.

So, what is his "why"?

His "Why" Is to Advance the Kingdom of God Every Time

Let's start with the big picture: Jesus makes his "why" so clear in the story in Matthew when he attends a large party thrown by Matthew. While being judged and ridiculed by the Pharisees for associating with such sinners (or as we would say in the Midwest, "hooligans"), Jesus states his mission statement like he's dropping a mic: "I have come to seek and save the lost."

So, already we see that his mission is different than ours. We come to seek and save ourselves. We pray to bless and better ourselves. Jesus comes to seek and save the lost.

Author Lee Strobel spent years researching miracles for his book *The Case for Miracles*. He points out that 93 percent of all people claim to have witnessed a miracle. And while that number seems to be excessive—and these "miracles" are often coincidences that we project onto God—Lee further clarifies what a miracle is, using a definition from philosophy professor Richard Purtill: "A miracle is an event brought about by the power of God that is a temporary exception to the ordinary course of nature, for the purpose of showing that God has acted in history."

So why does God do *these* types of miracles? When interviewed on the *Quick to Listen* podcast on December 20, 2019, he says that most documented miracles are seen in places where the gospel is just beginning to break forth. Much like with Jesus's ministry, his miracles were a way to prove that his words were worth listening to.

Strobel goes on to cite a study done in Mozambique, a place where the gospel is beginning to catch fire:

Researchers went into the remote areas and they said, "Bring us your blind and bring us your deaf." And so they did. And these are people with severe hearing or vision loss. And they tested them right on the spot, scientifically, to determine their level of vision and level of hearing. Then, immediately after that, they were prayed for in the name of Jesus by people who had a track record of God using them in healings, and then they were immediately scientifically tested again. In virtually every case, there was improvement. In some cases, extraordinary improvement.

So they went to Brazil, which is another place where miracles are clustering because the gospel is breaking into a new area. They did the same kind of experiment. Guess what? They got the same kinds of results.

So this is a valid scientific study that has been published in a secular, scientific, peer-reviewed medical journal. Strobel asked the researcher, Dr. Candace Brown, "What does this tell you?" And she said, "It's not fakery, it's not fraud, it's not people under the effects of emotionalism or whatever. Something is going on."

Does this mean these are the only conditions in which God says yes? Not at all. We all have seen evidence of God leveraging miracles in scenarios different than just places like Brazil and Mozambique. But advancing the kingdom of God is always part of God's why.

So what does this have to do with my waiting on God? Should I just give up praying for my daughter's chemistry test or my dying father's health? Not at all. But while we wait, a good question to ponder would be, "Is this something God would want to say yes to?"

Sometimes His "Why" Is to Be Generous Rather than Fair

We all want a life that is fair. From our early years, we cry out to our parents, "That's not fair." To our employers and government officials, we cry out, "But that's not fair." Part of this outcry is the result of living with the blessing of a bill of rights in America. Not everyone has this. We assume that all of us should be treated equally. However, this is not just an American problem. People throughout history have desired fair treatment as a simple human right, even back in Jesus's day. Though they lived with the Roman boot on their neck, they still desired things to be fair. Jesus tells a story explaining this very challenge.

A landowner hires day laborers at a rate of $50 a day. They start at 8:00 a.m. Then, he hires more workers at 12:00 p.m. Then, some more are hired at 4:00 p.m. When 5:00 p.m. hits, they all line up for their pay. The guys who worked the full day get their $50, not a problem. However, the workers all raise an eyebrow when the guys who showed up at noon receive the same pay. While I'm sure they were confused, they may have been thinking, "Okay, I guess we can overlook that." But when the slackers who showed up at 4:00, an hour before quitting time, get the $50 from the landowner, the guys who started at 8:00 begin to flip out. The workers cry out "That's not fair" to the owner. The landowner then responds: "'Is it against the law for me to do what I want with my money? Should you be jealous because I am kind to others?' So those who are last now will be first then, and those who are first will be last" (Matt. 20:15–16 NLT).

I have to be honest. I tend to side with the guys who started at 8:00 a.m. "This isn't fair." And, often, I see this come up in my prayer life. When the blessings of others look better than mine, I tend to cry, "God, this is not fair." I pray for our church to grow and thrive. I pray for success and good fortune. I pray for things to work out for my good. However, in these moments, I'm reminded that my "why" isn't always the same as God's "why."

I've been a pastor for over twenty-five years. I went to Bible college and seminary and have worked faithfully in the church every day in my life. However, sometimes when I see a guy who jumps in as a second career, with no training or hard knocks, and rises to meteoric success in ministry, it can really bother me. I know that sounds ridiculous. But when I see people like this on social media touting all the amazing things God is doing in just one year of ministry verses my twenty-five plus years, my mind can easily slip into, "Lord, it doesn't seem fair." It's in these moments that I hear Jesus say: "Should you be jealous because I am kind to others?"

Jesus seems to say my "why" should aim to be generous . . . not equal. And, unfortunately, this does not always feel fair.

Sometimes His "Why" Is to Restore Community

One of the most common things Christians pray for is physical healing. We pray to have our health restored; we pray for loved ones to be healed of cancer; we pray for the effects of a lifetime of poor eating and lack of exercise to be reversed; we even pray for a good night's sleep. I think that most of our prayers can be summed up into these three phrases: "Help me, bless me, and protect me. (Oh, and my loved ones too.)"

And when we look at the way Jesus responded to requests, we tend to assume he is all for that. He restores sight; he helps people walk; he removes skin diseases; and he even brings people back from the dead. So, why wouldn't we pray for complete physical healing and perfect living conditions at all times?

I host a weekly podcast, and recently I had a chance to interview Dr. Mark E. Moore, author, professor, and pastor. I asked him about the things Jesus said yes to, and he reminded us that Jesus's healings were never to bring about complete physical perfection. In other words, even though Lazarus comes back to life, he will still die again. Even though Jesus heals the woman with an issue of blood, she still would most likely have vitamin deficiency, tooth decay, and other first-century ailments. Jesus healed people to restore them to community. Lepers hadn't seen their families for years. This woman hadn't been intimate with her husband for years and was not allowed near the temple. Many blind and lame beggars were left on their own and unable to participate in their community. And now, all of them had been restored to their friends and family. Jesus's "why" seems to be less about "Yes, you asked me nicely," or "Yes, let me make your life perfect and trouble free," but more about "Let me restore you to community." As was said in the creation story, "It is not good for man to be alone."

While I know my prayers now are often to alleviate suffering, maybe my prayers should be more about restoring community. Now, this isn't to say that God doesn't cure cancer and heal the broken and prevent car wrecks. But he has a bigger "why" in mind. Perhaps my prayer should be more about understanding his "why" and yielding to it rather than just demanding my ease of momentary suffering. So, here's the question we all want to have answered: How did that restore community?

- I prayed for my daughter to be healed and she died. How did that restore community?
- I prayed for my wife to be restored from cancer, and she still died. How did that restore community?
- I prayed for safe travels, but we still had a car wreck and lost my son. How did that restore community?

Here is the hardest answer of all: sometimes, as much as we try to align with his "why," we may never know why.

In 1 Thessalonians 4:13, the apostle Paul tells Christians that they should "not grieve like people who have no hope" (NLT). This is written after some of the members of the Thessalonian church had recently died.

Paul wants to be perfectly clear: believers in Jesus Christ do not grieve over death as the rest of the world does. We hate death—we recognize it as the unnatural result of sin and the fall that it is—but we also know that for Christians, death is not the end of the story, but the beginning of eternity and wholeness with God.

The great comfort for believers who have had Christian loved ones perish—even children—is that the end is not truly the end. In verse 16, Paul goes on to say, referencing Christ's return: "For the Lord himself will descend from heaven with a cry of command, with the voice of an archangel, and with the sound of the trumpet of God. And the dead in Christ will rise first" (1 Thess. 4:16 ESV). From whence comes our hope in the face of death? Our dead brothers and sisters will rise again at the last day. In fact, all of 1 Corinthians chapter 15 is about the glorious promise of resurrection for all who have repented of their sins and placed their faith in Jesus Christ. This promise is so great, and the hope it presents so grand, that we can boldly taunt death, "Where, O death, is your victory? Where, O death, is your sting?" (1 Cor. 15:55).

This is where many of us go wrong. We think if we'd just prayed harder, then our loved one would not have died. But the problem is not in the passion of our zeal but in the object of our faith. To cling tightly with both hands to God's promise of final resurrection is right and necessary. Jesus has promised that healing will come—that there will be a day when death is no more—but it's not here yet.

That is why Paul does not say to the grieving Thessalonians, "Have you tried praying harder or singing more to bring them back?" No. He tells them to put their hope in the future resurrection, which was actually promised by God.

I am learning the hard way that prayer is not a wish that if you just cross your fingers hard enough, close your eyes tight enough, and work yourself up into enough of an emotional frenzy then maybe, just maybe, God will answer it. Christian prayer that God answers is a petition to the Almighty of the universe for aid made in accordance with his character and promises.

Christian prayer may come through tears and pleading, but it is characterized by a quiet confidence that God will do just as he has promised and by a heart that whispers "thy will be done"—even, and especially, during exceedingly tragic circumstances. God is our rock. We are not in control, and this is good news.

Indeed, believers in Jesus Christ do not grieve as those without hope. Because our hope is rooted in a promise from God to us: the bodily resurrection of the saints. But just as we do not grieve as those without hope, we also should not hope as those without a promise. Many of us hang our hopes on promises God has never made to us. He has not promised that our lives in this world will not be marked by pain, suffering, and death. But he has promised that one day, suffering will cease. As the apostle John wrote in exile on the island of Patmos, "He will wipe away every tear from their eyes, and death shall be no more, neither shall there be mourning, nor crying, nor pain anymore, for the former things have passed away" (Rev. 21:4 ESV).

Sometimes he restores community with us on earth, and sometimes he brings others into community with him in heaven.

The best way to know if it's his "why" is to simply ask him. Then what? Glad you asked.

Discussion Questions

1. Have you ever defined your "why" when it comes to your relationships?

2. If someone were to read your prayer journal and determine what God's "why" is, what would they say?

3. What prayers could you start praying that are in line with God advancing his gospel?

4. What prayers could you pray to be generous to others?

5. What prayers could you pray to restore community?

Next Steps

1. Take time for the next week to only pray prayers that are in line with God's "why."

2. Listen to Episode 78 on *The Rusty George Podcast*: "An interview with Dr. Mark E. Moore."

Prayers to Align with the "Why"

"The heavens declare the glory of God; the skies proclaim the work of his hands. Day after day they pour forth speech; night after night they reveal knowledge. They have no speech, they use no words; no sound is heard from them. Yet their voice goes out into all the earth, their words to the ends of the world." (Ps. 19:1–4)

"Hear my voice when I call, LORD; be merciful to me and answer me. My heart says of you, 'Seek his face!' Your face, LORD, I will seek. Do not hide your face from me, do not turn your servant away in anger; you have been my helper." (Ps. 27:7–9)

"Taste and see that the LORD is good; blessed is the one who takes refuge in him." (Ps. 34:8)

"You, God, are my God, earnestly I seek you; I thirst for you, my whole being longs for you, in a dry and parched land where there is no water. I have seen you in the sanctuary and beheld your power and your glory." (Ps. 63:1–2)

"Praise our God, all peoples, let the sound of his praise be heard; he has preserved our lives and kept our feet from slipping. For you, God, tested us; you refined us like silver. . . . we went through fire and water, but you brought us to a place of abundance." (Ps. 66:8–10, 12)

5

Yield the "How"

I was young, but not *that* young. Old enough to know better, but young enough to try. Our hometown college basketball team was in the NCAA Tournament, appropriately known as "March Madness," and they were on the brink of reaching the Final Four. A level previously unreached by our team and affectionately thought of as the promised land of college basketball (especially for a small-town school like ours). But, I had hope; and more than that, I had prayer.

While my parents watched the game, I quietly crept out of the room to go and pray. I felt like a superhero ducking out of sight to put on my cape. I would save our city by leveraging God.

I had heard in Sunday school that we should pray and not doubt:

> But when you ask, you must believe and not doubt, because the one who doubts is like a wave of the sea, blown and tossed by the wind. That person should not expect to receive anything from the Lord. Such a person is double-minded and unstable in all they do. (James 1:6–8)

I would not waiver. I would not be double-minded or unstable. My faith was resolute.

I got the family Bible out of the cabinet and placed it on a coffee table. I knelt before it and laid hands on it. Then, I began praying for our team to win. Surely this would work. After all, my hands were on the Bible and my knees were on the ground.

Despite all my best efforts, they lost. I guess someone else was doing the same thing for the opposing team. Maybe they prayed things in their prayers that I must have missed. Perhaps sack cloth or rosary beads?

I'd like to say that I've outgrown such displays, but truth be told, I still have my "repertoire" that I think will work. My unique way of getting God's attention and leveraging his favor. What is yours?

Maybe attend church on Sunday . . . then pray? Maybe you pray for longer than usual. Perhaps you ask others to pray, even call the church and ask them to pray. Maybe you fast. Maybe you lie on your face for hours pleading before God. All of these are great. And biblical. And should not be discounted. But what if they do more for our minds than they do for our answers?

For many of us, our fear is that our answers to prayers are based on a secret code. Similar to when we try to log on to one of the thirty thousand things in our lives that need a password. We try the usuals, then we remember they made us update our password; now we are trying everything we can possibly remember—kids' birthdays, graduation date, friends, streets we lived on, mother's maiden name, favorite pet—all while crossing our fingers and hoping for the best.

I do this with God too. What mixture of crying, "Father, please," kneeling, begging, and laying hands on the Bible do I need to make my prayers go through? But could it be that our methods aren't really the issue? What if it has more to do with our motives?

As discussed in the last chapter, aligning with God's "why" is important . . . but so is the "how." Not so much how we ask, but yielding to how he answers. I find that breaking my habits of thinking I can manipulate God with how I ask is not too difficult—kneeling, hand on the Bible, etc. What can be very difficult to give up is my obsession with how he answers. After all, I have a prayer . . . and a plan. And I'd like God to fulfill both.

The Jewish patriarch Joseph had to come to terms with this. He was given a dream that showed his brothers bowing down before him one day. As any teenage kid would do, he decided to share this with his brothers, thinking they'd be overjoyed for him. Not so much. This revelation resulted in him being sold into slavery. This began an eighteen-year journey of banishment, exile, and servitude that landed him in Pharaoh's prison. And then, in a matter of moments, he was whisked from the prison and was standing in the palace where he was given the keys to the kingdom. Just a few years later, his brothers would be kneeling at his feet begging for food. As Timothy Keller, pastor and theologian, phrases it, "God will either give us what we ask or give us what we would have asked if we knew everything he knows." It wasn't the timing Joseph had imagined, but he was forced to surrender the "how" of God's promise. He had to yield the "how."

Challenging Jesus

How God chooses to do things seems to be a question for all of us. It was frequently a point of contention for those who were around Jesus.

In Matthew 12, we read the people are getting restless. Now Jesus has claimed to be able to cast out demons and the teachers of the law want to see some proof. This has actually been asked for before. Despite all the miracles Jesus has already performed, when Jesus starts saying he has power over death and demons, they'd like to see some proof. Is this really the Messiah or just a magician? To be fair, what's the harm in Jesus doing a couple extra miracles to ease their minds? I think you and I would probably oblige. But not Jesus.

> A wicked and adulterous generation asks for a sign!
> But none will be given it except the sign of the
> prophet Jonah. For as Jonah was three days and three
> nights in the belly of a huge fish, so the Son of Man
> will be three days and three nights in the heart of the
> earth. (Matt. 12:39–40)

This was not out of the question. Any time someone claimed to be the Messiah, they required some verification. But Jesus is saying, "Not yet. It will come, and it will look different than you expect. But come Easter morning, you'll have your sign."

Even on the day of the crucifixion, people are still taunting him for a sign. "You've saved others, save yourself!" "Come down from the cross!" The humanity in me would say, "I'll show you!" But Jesus is focused on not just the "why," but also the "how." While he could come down from the cross and blow their minds, he can stay on the cross and save the world. Easter is coming.

It is interesting that this is the tactic Satan uses to try to rattle Jesus. "Turn these stones into bread," "Throw yourself off the temple," or even, "Bow down to me." Because if you do, I'll give up my hold on humanity. Don't the ends justify the means? And yet, Jesus is resolute. "I'm trusting my Father with not just the 'why,' but also the 'how.'"

Even Jesus's cousin, John the Baptist, had to wrestle with this. He had been tasked with preparing the way for the Lord, and he did it. He was baptizing people, telling them to "Repent for the Kingdom of God was near." And then when Jesus arrived, he said, "Behold the Lamb of God." "He must become greater, I must become less." He had lived out his "why." He was to prepare the way for the Lord.

He even had the auspicious responsibility of baptizing Jesus. He tried to get out of the how of this by saying, "I shouldn't baptize you, but you me." To which Jesus said, "'Let it be so now; it is proper for us to do this to fulfill all righteousness.' Then John consented" (Matt. 3:15).

Not long after this, John will have his greatest crisis of faith. After months of John publicly teaching that a new King of the Jews is here, the current self-proclaimed King of the Jews, King

Herod, will take issue with this. Particularly his wife. And she forces her husband to arrest John.

While in prison, John hears about all the miracles Jesus is performing and is wondering why he isn't helping his cousin get out of prison. *Could he have been mistaken? Did he get it wrong?*

"When John, who was in prison, heard about the deeds of the Messiah, he sent his disciples to ask him, "Are you the one who is to come, or should we expect someone else?'" (Matt. 11:3). *Is it really you? Are you really God in the flesh? Because, I assumed that God who called me to do this job would protect me.*

John is asking the same question we do. When things go badly, we wonder. It rattles one of the earliest prayers we learn: "God is great, God is good, let us thank him for our food." So, is God's silence an indicator that either God isn't *great* or that God isn't *good*? Jesus answered: "Go back and report to John what you hear and see: The blind receive sight, the lame walk, those who have leprosy are cleansed, the deaf hear, the dead are raised, and the good news is proclaimed to the poor. Blessed is anyone who does not stumble on account of me" (Matt. 11:4–6).

Jesus is saying to the Pharisees, the soldiers, and now John the Baptist, "Trust my father with the *why*, but also the *how*."

Now what about us?

Yield the "How"

Like you probably do, I keep a prayer list. I used to write it in some fancy prayer journal, but now I use the Notes app on my phone. It's not elaborate, but it works. I simply write the request, and that's it. I'll go back and read over them almost every day and utter a simple prayer for these things. It seems rude to just read a list to God, so I'll often add my own suggestions as to how these things can and should be done.

"God, Becki is sick. Will you heal her by removing the cancer?"

"God, Mark is looking for work. Will you give him the job he recently interviewed for?"

"God, my daughter has a test today. Will you help her ace it and get a massive scholarship so I won't have to pay for college?" (Well, maybe not quite this self-serving . . . maybe.)

I surrender that God is sovereign and that his plan, whatever that might be, is best. (The "why.") But what I struggle with is the "how." I'd like things to be done the way I would if I were God.

This had to be a struggle in the first church in the first century. Imagine how exciting things must have been. The resurrected Jesus has said the "why" and the "what": "Go and make disciples of all nations, baptizing them in the name of the Father and of the Son and of the Holy Spirit, and teaching them to obey everything I have commanded you" (Matt. 28:19–20).

Then about ten days later, that's exactly what they did. Peter shares the good news to all who had gathered in Jerusalem for the feast of Pentecost, and three thousand people respond to the altar call. They begin to share belongings, take care of one another, and live out their mission. Happily ever after, right?

They forgot the "go into all the world" part. So, when persecution breaks out and they have to flee Jerusalem, everyone is praying for this to end. This is not their idea of "how" to do church. But God uses this to help them take the good news from Jerusalem to Judea, Samaria, and the world. It seems very similar to what the church experienced through shelter in place during Easter of 2020. While thousands of church buildings were closed, the church opened up online and, thus, in countless homes. Our church and many others experienced a higher attendance than ever before. At first thought, we might have said "Church is closed on Easter," but the truth was the church had just left the building. It was actually having a bigger impact than ever before. Did God cause COVID-19? No, but God used it.

What about when one of the leaders of that early church, James, is martyred. They have to wonder, *God, is this how you are going to build your church? By allowing its leaders to die?* And what about the fact that James and his brother John were two of Jesus's closest friends and one is killed and the other is allowed to live a long life? Why one and not the other? *God, is this how you advance your kingdom? It's not how I would.*

Part of our prayers must be surrendering "how I would do things if I were God."

It's as if our role is to lay out our need before God, but yield the manner in which he meets the need. He may have something else in mind, we know he has a bigger plan than ours, and we must come to terms with how he will finish his grand redemption story. There is no need to doubt that we've been heard, and no need to doubt that God will answer; we only need to reconcile that it might not be the way we had hoped.

What Is Your "How" to Yield?

"God, you want me to live in community with others. . . . I'd like to have that with a beautiful, wealthy, and servant-minded spouse. I'll leave their name up to you."

But, what if God chooses to use you to be a friend to those in need, serve those less fortunate, or live in community with a group of people with special needs?

"God, you know my basic needs are food, clothing, and shelter. So, when it comes to shelter, could that be in a quiet neighborhood with large lots, picturesque views, and parks and pools."

But, what if God chooses to give you a place to live, but it's in a less desirable part of town? It may not bring the luxury you desire, but the price point may bring peace of mind each month when you pay the mortgage.

"God, please heal my mother."

But, what if God chooses to heal her by using this sickness to bring her and others in your family to salvation? Thus, her healing is by waking up in heaven, and you and your family knowing you'll be with her one day soon.

The patriarchs of our faith would use a phrase that sums it up: facing the dark night of the soul. It's that feeling of going through a dark tunnel unable to see the end, but trusting that God is with you . . . even if you can't see him. As painful as this journey can be, it is during these moments that our senses are heightened to our need for God, our own frailty, and life's uncertainty. We are slowly weaned off pleasure and comfort as our ultimate satisfaction and we come to a place where all we want is the presence of Jesus. In other words, sometimes Jesus isn't all we need until he's all we've got. It's in these moments that our pride can turn into humility, our greed can become simplicity, our wrath gives way to contentment, and our envy settles into joy. I must be honest: these are not my favorite moments in life's journey—but they are the most transformative.

As a pastor of a church, one of the common things I pray for is church growth. The prayer has several different looks, but it's all the same. "God, use our church to bless this community." "God, help people in our city to come to faith in you." "God, will you help bring a lot of new people to church this weekend?" One day, I was struck with this thought, which must have only come from God himself: "Would you be okay if I blessed the city, the community, and the lost . . . but did so through another church?" Uh . . . I plead the fifth.

> Sometimes Jesus isn't all we need until he's all we've got.

So, when I watched God use new churches that would spring up and grow rapidly, I faced my own dark night of the soul. *God, why are you using them and not us? God, have we done something wrong? God, where did you go? Did you change churches?*

God did what God does. He forcefully advances his Kingdom in this world in ways that are not always like mine. And even though I'm okay with his "why" . . . waiting allows me to get comfortable with his "how," as well.

Discussion Questions

1. Do you struggle more with *if* God answers prayers or *how* God answers prayers?

2. What is a prayer you often pray for which you are holding on to the "how"?

3. While you are waiting on God, are you becoming less particular about how he might answer you?

4. Describe a time in the past when God gave you a yes, but not in a way you had hoped.

5. What if every prayer you prayed, you said not just "your will be done," but also "your way be done"?

Next Steps

1. Brainstorm all the ways God could say yes to your request that might be different than what you had hoped.

2. In your prayers this week, spend less time telling God how you want things done and more time asking for him to make you aware of what he is currently doing.

Prayers to Yield the "How"

"Show me your ways, LORD, teach me your paths. Guide me in your truth and teach me, for you are God my Savior, and my hope is in you all day long." (Ps. 25:4–5)

"Good and upright is the LORD; therefore he instructs sinners in his ways. He guides the humble in what is right and teaches them his way. All the ways of the LORD are loving and faithful toward those who keep the demands of his covenant." (Ps. 25:8–10)

"You have searched me, LORD, and you know me. You know when I sit and when I rise; you perceive my thoughts from afar. You discern my going out and my lying down; you are familiar with all my ways. Before a word is on my tongue you, LORD, know it completely. You hem me in behind and before, and you lay your hand upon me. Such knowledge is too wonderful for me, too lofty for me to attain." (Ps. 139:1–6)

"Search me, God, and know my heart; test me and know my anxious thoughts. See if there is any offensive way in me, and lead me in the way everlasting." (Ps. 139:23–24)

"Answer me quickly, LORD; my spirit fails. Do not hide your face from me or I will be like those who go down to the pit. Let the morning bring me word of your unfailing love, for I have put my trust in you. Show me the way I should go, for to you I entrust my life. . . . Teach me to do your will, for you are my God; may your good Spirit lead me on level ground." (Ps. 143:7–8, 10)

6

Do the Next Right Thing

George Müller was a prayer rock star.

Müller was the director of the Ashley Down orphanages in Bristol, England. During his lifetime, he cared for 10,024 orphans and established 117 schools, which offered Christian education to over 100,000 children. Through all this, Müller never asked for money. All of what he accomplished was the result of prayer and donations. For example, on one occasion, he and the children were praying for breakfast while sitting at a table with not only nothing on the table, but no food even in the home. As they finished praying, a baker knocked on the door with fresh bread to feed everyone. Then the milkman walked up and gave them plenty of fresh milk because his cart broke down in front of the orphanage. Most of us will never pray this type of prayer for food. In fact, most of my prayers for food are "God, please help this meal full of fat and sugar somehow bless my body." In Müller's autobiography, he says that he can document over one thousand prayers answered like this. Like I said, Müller was a prayer rock star.

George was crossing the Atlantic in August 1877 when his ship ran into thick fog. He explained to the captain that he needed to be in Quebec by the following afternoon, but the Captain said that he was slowing the ship down for safety and that Müller's appointment would have to be missed. Müller asked to use the chartroom to pray for the lifting of the fog. The captain followed him down, claiming it would be a waste of time. After Müller prayed a very simple prayer, the captain started to pray, but Müller stopped him; partly because of the captain's unbelief, but mainly because he believed the prayer had already been answered. Müller said, "Captain, I have known my Lord for more than fifty years and there is not one instance that I have failed to have an audience with the King. Get up, Captain, for you will find that the fog has gone." When the two men went back to the bridge, they found the fog had lifted, and Müller was able to keep his appointment.

When we read about lives like Müller's, we are tempted to think, *Is that even possible?* Do those kinds of prayer requests even exist today? Or is Müller just a rare breed that has all but died off by now? For me, it is easy to slip into a bit of a spiritual malaise, thinking, *If that's what it takes for God to answer my prayers, I'm sunk.* Inside, I wonder, *This must be what it means to have faith . . . and I am not anywhere near that.*

The author of Hebrews tells us: "And it is impossible to please God without faith. Anyone who wants to come to him must believe that God exists and that he rewards those who sincerely seek him" (Heb. 11:6 NLT). When I read about George Müller, I think, *If that's the standard of faith, then I fall way short.* This also must be what Peter felt when he got out of the boat.

It's late at night when the disciples are in a boat on the Sea of Galilee. They are making their way from one side of the lake to another, and Jesus says, "I'll catch up with you." What must they have been thinking when Jesus said, "I'll catch up with you"? After all, they are the ones taking the short cut, going by boat across the lake rather than walking around on the shore. Is Jesus going to kayak out to them? But, as Jesus does, he decides to walk on the water. Jesus is funny that way.

Not only are the disciples already on edge due to a storm and the fierce waves, but now suddenly there is someone walking on the water. Imagine the fear of the disciples when in the midst of bailing water and trying to get to shore, they look up and see a figure on the waves. They all must have been wondering if someone spiked their canteens. Their first thought is, *It's a ghost!* Jesus can see their fear and begins to calm them: "It's me!" To which Peter responds, "If it's you, tell me to come to you." Is Peter daring him? Does Peter doubt that it might be him? Does Peter know anyone else who is able to walk on water? All questions for heaven when I buy him a cup of coffee. Or a fish sandwich.

Regardless of Peter's motives or assumptions, he is the only one to ask. And he is the only one to get out of the boat. He starts by issuing a dare: "Lord, if it's you . . . tell me to come to you on the water" (Matt. 14:28). Not sure what Peter is trying to vet here by daring Jesus to call him out, but Jesus responds, saying, "Come on out!" Knowing Peter the way we do, I doubt he carefully put one leg over the side and then the other. I'm sure he just jumped overboard as if to say, "Okay, I'm calling your bluff!" And guess what, he stuck the landing. He was standing on water. He began to take some steps and all was well, until the waves swelled and the wind picked up. And that was enough to push Peter's faith toward fear. His next step toward Jesus was more like the lunge of a child falling into the water grasping for their dad! In the sinking and flailing about, he cries out to Jesus to save him. Jesus grabs his hand, pulls him close, and says, "Why did you doubt?" (v. 31).

When Jesus says, "You have so little faith," some have theorized that maybe Jesus was looking at the disciples who stayed in the boat. After all, even though Peter sank, he was the only one to get out of the boat. Peter's act of climbing out of the boat in the middle of a stormy lake—with no life jacket—was a big risk. Even if it was short-lived. If this is what it takes to see God work . . . I'm sunk (pun intended.)

Author and professor James Bryan Smith takes a different approach when it comes to stories like George Müller and how we understand them. His mentor and friend Dallas Willard would teach that faith is an extension of knowledge based on knowledge, meaning faith is how I act based on what I know. Once James was able to fully grasp this concept, it felt as if a huge weight was lifted off his shoulders. He began to understand that faith is not trying to believe something you don't truly believe in. The more we walk with God, the more we come to know God; the deeper our

> Faith is an extension of knowledge based on knowledge.

relationship with God is in the way that he acts, the more we're able to take those steps in faith. In this way, we can grow in our faith because faith is acting on what you believe.

If I can attempt to take Smith's explanation of Willard's teaching and dumb it down even more, it's like *Indiana Jones and the Last Crusade*. (How's that?)

Those that have seen the movie may remember toward the end, Jones has to pass a series of tests in order to get to the Holy Grail, and thus save his father. The last test is to cross an open chasm that appears to have no bridge. A leap of faith is required. Once Indy takes a step, he finds the bridge. How could he do it?

Indy's step of faith was not a sudden act. He did not come to this quickly. Over the course of the movie, we learn that Indy's relationship with his father had been strained at best. And while searching for the Holy Grail, Indy is forced to rely on recorded instructions in a book of clues. But they aren't just random notes—this book was written by his father. Staring out over the chasm, Indy could close his eyes and take the biggest step in his life because he could trust in what his father knew.

Indy's faith was, as Dallas Willard would say, "an extension of knowledge based on knowledge." Peter discovered faith in the same way. When he first meets Jesus, Peter says, "Get away from me; I'm not worthy to be in your presence." But after years of following Jesus and seeing him prove not just his power but also his acceptance of all those "unworthy," Peter has enough knowledge and trust to get out of the boat.

So how does that give me hope when I sense silence from heaven? What am I supposed to do with this while I am waiting on God? I've prayed my guts out and still nothing. I'm left with the voices in my head telling me, *It's your fault. You don't have enough faith. God is waiting on you to believe more. Try harder.* If faith is acting on what I believe . . . am I just not believing enough?

One day, an official came to Jesus asking for a miracle. This official was quite possibly a servant of Herod. Most likely a Gentile. Not a Jew, not a Jesus follower, and certainly not a disciple. All he knows is this rabbi seems to have magical powers. He says, "Will you come to my house and heal my son?" This would have been unheard of for a Jewish rabbi to enter the home of a Gentile Roman official. There is no promise of duty or servanthood. There is no confession of faith in Jesus as the Messiah. There is nothing that seems to indicate he is "good enough" to gain Jesus's mercy. He just wants the miracle.

Sometimes when I pray, I quietly hope that God will grant my request without asking too many questions. Much like when my kids ask for money and hope I don't ask what for. This guy just wants the favor. The miracle. And to be honest, sometimes so do I. I pray for good grades for my kids . . . so that they get scholarships to schools. I pray for good weather . . . so that it won't mess up my plans for the weekend. I pray for good fortune for others . . . so they might bless the church. I hope Jesus doesn't know how self-serving my prayers can be, but who am I kidding?

Jesus responds to this man a bit harshly: "Will you never believe in me unless you see miraculous signs and wonders?" (John 4:48 NLT). This answer is to not just this man, but also the crowd. They've been asking for more signs and wonders. This won't be the last time Jesus pushes back on miracle hunters. Jesus wants us to believe in him for who he is, not just for what he does. These miracles were given as evidence when John the Baptist had questions, but they will never fully satisfy the thrill seekers.

That being said, why does this poor guy catch some of Jesus's rebuke? Isn't that a bit harsh? After all, his son is on his deathbed and he comes to Jesus begging for some help. Perhaps it's because this man's faith is a bit shortsighted. He thinks Jesus must actually be physically present for healing to happen. And he thinks Jesus can only prevent death, not raise the dead.

The man begins to plead with Jesus: "Sir, come down before my child dies" (John 4:49). You have to admire the guy's persistence. He won't take no for an answer. So Jesus gives him an answer—but also a task: "Go back home. Your son will live!" (John 4:50 NLT). You can almost hear the man responding, "What? No, you must come with me . . ." met with Jesus's assured reply: "Go home."

"But how do I know you will heal him? What if it doesn't take? What if there's poor reception or the call gets dropped? Shouldn't you come with me?"

"Go home."

We are not told how long the father waits before he leaves, but eventually he starts heading home. Wondering about his son, if this will work, if he will even see his son alive again.

Can you imagine how helpless this must have felt? Just go home? He came to get the teacher. He came to bring the doctor, and he's going home empty-handed. How will he face his wife? How will he face his son? At least if he had Jesus with him, he would have done all he could do. But now? He's got nothing but a prayer. Nothing but a hope. Nothing but a word of assurance. Jesus said to go. And the text tells us that he took Jesus at his word. So he went.

Yet on the way, he gets some good news from some of his servants. Jesus had healed his boy from some twenty miles away. And the father must be ecstatic. But like a typical guy, he wants to do some fact checking. I love his follow-up question:

> He asked them when the boy had begun to get better, and they replied, "Yesterday afternoon at one o'clock his fever suddenly disappeared!" Then the father realized that that was the very time Jesus had told him, "Your son will live." And he and his entire household believed in Jesus. (John 4:52–53 NLT)

When did this happen? Right when Jesus said it would.

Sometimes the best thing to do while we wait, is to just do the next right thing. For this man, the best thing to do was to go home. What might that be for you? This sentiment was summed up well in Disney Pixar's hit movie *Frozen 2*. (No judgment. I have two daughters. And okay, I like Olaf.) There is a scene in the movie where the characters are faced with surmounting challenges when things seem hopeless, wondering what to do next. They sing together about walking in the night and the need to do the next right thing. In the Spotify commentary track, singer Kristen Bell and songwriter Robert Lopez explain that the song "The Next Right Thing" is very much based on the death of director Chris Buck's son in 2013, right before the original film was released. Sometimes, the only thing you can do is pray . . . then do the next right thing.

If faith is knowledge based on what we know, sometimes all we know is the next right thing. George Müller had lived long enough and taken enough steps of faith that he had a greater knowledge of what would happen next. So the next right thing was for him to just pray. Keep going. Tell the captain of the ship to proceed.

Peter had seen enough of Jesus's works to know that walking on the water wasn't out of the realm of possibility for Jesus. What he did question was whether or not it was out of the realm of possibility for him. So when he did the next right thing in getting out of the boat, he didn't doubt Jesus's ability, but his own.

The royal official knew he was out of options to help his son. He had no faith, no supernatural gifting, but only the knowledge that this rabbi had some abilities beyond his own. So, he did the next right thing. He went to Jesus and then went home. And Jesus's answer went ahead of him.

So, what is the next right thing for you?

You've prayed for your marriage. You've begged God to "fix your spouse" or heal your heart. But nothing seems to change. Maybe the next right thing is to keep serving. To keep praying. To be the brightest reflection of Jesus's grace that you can be while you wait for Jesus's miracle to go before you.

You've prayed for your son. He's off the rails. Prodigal, you might say. You've asked God to bring him back to the faith of his youth, or to awaken him to the error of his ways. What's the next right thing? Tough love? Change the locks and cut him off. Or is it to go get him? He's felt rejected, so go show how loved and welcomed he is.

You're prayed for your finances. Nothing seems to work. Every job you seek that looks promising goes to someone else. Every call you try to make goes cold. Every pending sale falls through. You've asked God to give and fix and bail you out, but maybe the next right thing is to start cutting expenses. Consider moving. Ask what the bigger plan might be. Not just, "God, help me continue my current way of living," but ask, "God, what's the new normal you may be leading me toward?"

You've prayed for your failing health. You're not an invalid, but you are not healthy. You feel overwhelmed and discouraged by not being able to be the person you used to be. Your list of doctors is longer than your arm and your medications are so many it feels like another meal. So now what? Why won't God take this away? Maybe the next right thing is to start finding others worse off than you. People you can encourage, serve, take to doctor's appointments, or visit in the hospital.

You've prayed to find a friend. Thousands of social media followers, but you feel like no one knows you. Is there anyone who could encourage you? Support you? Pray for you? You've prayed to make a friend, but maybe the next right thing is to be a friend.

You've prayed for sobriety. You've wanted to break free from your addiction, but you are tempted everywhere you go. Will God ever take away the temptation? Maybe not. But you can find a group of others who are walking through the twelve steps together on a daily basis. Maybe the next right thing is to join them.

My friend Roy Mays reminded me of this. Roy was a pastor at a thriving megachurch when he got sick. He had no idea what it was. No doctor could diagnose it either. For the next several years, he went from doctor to doctor, hospital to clinic, and nothing could give him the answers or the healing he needed. Until one day, they finally clarified it as a very rare type of bone cancer. His condition was terminal. Roy shifted his focus. For the remaining months or years he had left, his prayers moved from *God heal me* to *God use me*. He traveled across the country speaking in churches, hospitals, universities, and local cancer support groups to encourage people that our God is still worth following, even when you can't see in the dark. By the time Roy was called home to be with Jesus, his impact had been greater in a few years with cancer than in the fifty years without. All by doing the next right thing.

Discussion Questions

1. Tell of a time when you had to seek out help.

2. How did you feel when you were waiting?

3. What would you have said to Jesus when he said, "Go home"?

4. What is the next right thing for you to do?

5. When will you start?

Next Steps

1. Go public with your next right thing.

2. Keep a list of others' next right things and hold each other accountable.

Prayers as You Do the Next Right Thing

"We wait in hope for the LORD; he is our help and our shield. In him our hearts rejoice, for we trust in his holy name. May your unfailing love be with us, LORD, even as we put our hope in you." (Ps. 33:20–22)

"Trust in the LORD and do good; dwell in the land and enjoy safe pasture. Take delight in the LORD, and he will give you the desires of your heart. Commit your way to the LORD; trust in him and he will do this: He will make your righteous reward shine like the dawn, your vindication like the noonday sun." (Ps. 37:3–6)

"Blessed is the one who trusts in the LORD, who does not look to the proud, to those who turn aside to false gods. Many, LORD my God, are the wonders you have done, the things you planned for us. None can compare with you; were I to speak and tell of your deeds, they would be too many to declare." (Ps. 40:4–5)

"You are my portion, LORD; I have promised to obey your words. I have sought your face with all my heart; be gracious to me according to your promise. I have considered my ways and have turned my steps to your statutes. I will hasten and not delay to obey your commands." (Ps. 119:57–60)

"Blessed are all who fear the LORD, who walk in obedience to him. You will eat the fruit of your labor; blessings and prosperity will be yours." (Ps. 128:1–2)

7

Share the Last 10 Percent

For all the times we catch our kids in a lie, they are often the most brutally honest of any of us.

One busy morning, my family was racing around to head out of the house. At the time, our girls were four and two, and getting their cooperation was not always an easy feat. That being said, we finally had them dressed, packed up with toys and dolls, and we were headed for the car. Our path outside took us from the kitchen, through the laundry room, and then out to the garage. My wife had been in the laundry room earlier in the morning sorting clothes into their proper piles before they made it into the washer. This usually ended up with about eight to ten piles of various shades and types of clothes. Even though we'd been married over a dozen years at this point, I still was stupefied as to why we needed so many piles. When I was single and in college, I had two piles: whites and everything else. I had never turned anything pink, and I had never lost a sock. She loves it when I bring that up. Nevertheless, when the four of us walked through the laundry room, all the nice neat piles of clothes had been stirred into one big pile. It looked as if the Tasmanian Devil had run through the room. Lorrie stopped and said to all of us, "Who did this?" I was trying not to be offended that I was included, and just as I was about to defend myself and throw the kids under the bus, our precious two-year-old daughter, Sidney, spoke up. With honesty and clarity and not a hint of aggression or animosity, she said, "I did it. And I did it on purpose."

I laughed probably more than I should have. My wife gave a brief reprimand to Sidney (and to me) and then once we got in the car, she started laughing too. And we've never forgotten that moment.

It was almost confessional. Let's skip the interrogation and the threatening. Let's not stand around and stare and wonder who will cop a plea. "I'll own it. I did it. I'm not proud of it, but I can't hide it. It was me."

There is something endearing about such honesty.

It seems like the older we get, the more we have to work at that type of honesty. We have a saying in our organization that we've adopted from other places. It is "Give me the last 10 percent." In other words, most of us are about 90 percent honest with each other. But it's the last 10 percent that is so crucial. It's in that final 10 percent where we get clear and real with one another.

It's from the last 10 percent that real change and understanding can happen. So why not go ahead and share it?

Think about your friends. You go to lunch, you talk about your life, you share your struggles, and often we say, "Oh that's too bad," or, "Of course you are right and he is wrong"; and then we get in the car and text one of the other friends we were with and say, "What are they thinking?" That's the last 10 percent. Sadly, often the last 10 percent is shared with everyone but the one who really needs to hear it.

Clearly, God is a fan of honesty. It made his top ten: "Thou shall not lie." And I think we'd all agree that being able to trust one another is crucial to a relationship. But what we often forget is that being truthful is not only helpful to the other person; it's helpful to us.

James says it this way in his letter to the early church: "Confess your sins to each other and pray for each other so that you may be healed. The prayer of a righteous person is powerful and effective" (James 5:16). In our confessing to one another, something happens in us: we are forever changed.

James is dealing with communities in which there was a great deal of social tension. So, what he is talking about is more than just a physical healing, but a relational healing as well. Christian remedies for fractured relationships are open confession of sin and mutual prayer. These actions promote transparency, support, and unity. Thus, when he says, "so that," he is referring to not just physical healing, but also a deeper spiritual healing of sin and broken relationships.

We like to focus on the second half of this verse. The original language says it best: "The effective prayer of a righteous man can accomplish much." So . . . what is effective? And what is righteous?

Righteous simply implies that our unconfessed sin can break down our connection with God. (More to come in another chapter on that one.) Effective is a confession that is put into action. Not just in word alone, but also in deed. I pray . . . then I work. Do the next right thing. But we must not miss the first part of this. Come clean. Be honest. Share the last 10 percent.

Wherever Jesus went, there seemed to be a crowd. And with a crowd came the Pharisees. While others showed up for hope and healing, the Pharisees showed up to judge and condemn. After all, they were the ones who had cornered the market on righteousness. How dare anyone move in on their turf. So one day, with a crowd of both those full of guilt and those full of themselves, Jesus told a story about two men who walk into the temple to pray. (I wonder if people started to laugh—like "Two men walk into a bar.") Jesus says, the first guy is a Pharisee. Rule keeping, law-abiding, morality policing. And he prays, "God, thank you that I'm not like the rest of society—cheaters, sinners, adulterers, or even this tax collector." It's almost like he's praying and looking around the room. Every Pharisee must have bristled at this—like Jesus had been eavesdropping on their prayers. The rest of the crowd must have been thinking, *Sounds about right.* Then the story continues: "The second guy is a tax collector (insert awkward laughter here). But his prayer is different. He cowers in the corner; he curls up in the fetal position and begs God for forgiveness. 'God, have mercy on me.'" You could probably cut the tension with a knife. Then Jesus drops this truth bomb: the Pharisee left with only his arrogance; the tax collector left with God's grace.

The contrast in these two characters is rather evident. One is humble; the other is not. The tax collector prays to God, while the Pharisee seems to pray to himself. The Pharisee doesn't even ask for anything, but just reports how good he's been. The tax collector, on the other hand, stands at a distance, recognizing his own unworthiness before God. He refuses to assume the normal posture of Jewish prayer—standing, looking up to heaven. Rather, he bows humbly, averts his gaze, and begs for mercy. "God, have mercy on me, a sinner" (Luke 18:13). In the original Greek it reads, "God, have mercy on me, *the* sinner!" Interesting how the Pharisee promotes himself as *the* righteous and the tax collector admits to being *the* sinner.

Many times, when I pray, I find myself attempting to read my résumé as *the* righteous, the one who deserves God's favor and blessing. After all, I've earned it. "God, you know how much I've given." "You know how good I've been." "You know how all the other guys go out after work and are never with their families." "You know how I always come home and take care of my family." And on and on and on.

But the one who receives mercy from God in Jesus's story does just the opposite. He comes clean. In fact, I'd venture to say that his honesty was seen as his righteousness. After all, there is no one righteous, according to Paul. But when we pray, our ability to share the last 10 percent is not only healing for us, but also music to God's ears.

Jesus is drawn to honesty.

Once again, we read about Jesus and the disciples in a boat on the Sea of Galilee. Something epic always happens when they are in a boat on the Sea of Galilee. If I were one of the disciples, I would start bracing myself for an encounter with the supernatural every time I boarded.

For years when reading these stories about this body of water, I always pictured something massive—the Mediterranean Sea, or at least Lake Michigan. But the Sea of Galilee is rather small. You can see to the other side at most spots. But based on where it sits between hills and mountains, and based on the type of weather it is prone to see, storms come up frequently and often without warning. And let's face it, the type of boats they had back then were hardly the kind to withstand heavy weather.

So here they are in a boat on the water, and things are so calm that Jesus goes to sleep. Jesus is so tired and goes into such deep REM sleep that he doesn't even wake up when a storm kicks up. The disciples have reached the point of fear. Most of the disciples were fishermen by trade, so a storm would have to be something of significance to cause them to panic. They are bailing water, shouting orders, trying to set the sail correctly; and they look over at Jesus, and he's sound asleep. Their words to Jesus are fascinating: "The disciples woke him up, shouting, 'Teacher, don't you care that we're going to drown?'" (Mark 4:38 NLT).

> They say nothing about Jesus's ability to *fix* their problem, but say everything about Jesus's *concern* about their problem.

They don't wake him with "Hey, can you calm the storm? Can you perform one of your miracles and fix this? Maybe cause our boat not to flood? Or perhaps just teleport us to the shore? Not sure how you do all those miracles, but one would be nice here." They say nothing about Jesus's ability to *fix* their problem, but say everything about Jesus's *concern* about their problem.

"Don't you care?" Let's be honest. That's what we all want to know sometimes, isn't it?

"God, it's been six months, and I can't find a job. Don't you care?"

"God, she's been through three rounds of chemo, and the cancer keeps coming back. Don't you care?"

"God, we've tried for years to get pregnant... Don't you care?"

Jesus is not offended. Jesus does not roll over and go back to sleep. Jesus is drawn to honesty. Jesus leans in for the last 10 percent.

I'm comforted by the words of Christine Caine when she says, "Even if people have disappointed you, or circumstances have not turned out like you hoped or prayed, know that God is with you, cares for you, and loves you. He is working on these things together for your good at this very moment."

Another time, a man comes to Jesus asking for healing for his son. The disciples had tried, but were unable to assist. The boy was in dire straits due to being possessed by a demon. This demon would cause physical harm to the child, hurling him into water or a fire trying to kill him. The man turns to Jesus and says, "Have mercy on us and help us, if you can!" (Mark 9:22 NLT). Notice the lack of perfect faith here: "if you can."

Jesus digs into that a bit by saying, "What do you mean, 'If I can?' Anything is possible if a person believes" (v. 23 NLT).

Can I just say I find this again encouraging? If my fear of seeing God answer my prayers is based on my lack of perfect faith, I need not worry. Because once again, Jesus responds to something more than just faith. He responds to honesty.

"The father instantly cried out, 'I do believe, but help me overcome my unbelief!'" (v. 24 NLT).

Talk about sharing the last 10 percent.

"I believe . . . as much as I can. Help me with what's missing."

So, what do you do when you are waiting on God? Get real. Be honest. And share the last 10 percent.

Isn't this what many of us fear? We fear if we are too direct, we'll show disrespect. We fear if we are too aggressive, we'll scare him off. We fear if we cut to the chase and skip the small talk, it will seem too transactional. But it's clear that while Jesus bristles at our selfish demands, he is drawn to our vulnerable honesty. It's the difference between "Show us a sign" and "Help me overcome my unbelief."

In *Traveling Mercies*, Anne Lamott summarizes the best two kinds of prayer that anyone can pray. Her first prayer is simply the word "help." This is our way of saying to God, "I can't do this. I'm at my wits' end. I'm out of options. Help me." It's a word of humility and vulnerability. I'm at my wits' end. I have nothing left. This is me.

Reminds me of what C. S. Lewis famously said in *The Problem of Pain*: "God whispers to us in our pleasure but shouts to us in our pain." Some of the greatest self-discoveries are a result of us coming to the end of our rope. And it is here that God has our attention. And we have his. Help!

Lamott goes on to say the second word is "thanks." We might be saying thank you for coming through. Thank you for listening. Thank you for being patient with me and not smiting me as I spoke. Thank you.

Everything between those two phrases is just filler. So, what is it that you really think and feel but have yet to say? This might be something to consider while you sit in God's waiting room.

It's not that our honesty gets a yes; but it does get us whole. Again, as Lewis says, "Prayer doesn't change God. It changes me."

Come Out of the Shadows

A woman with a medical condition has great faith thinking that if she just touches the garment of Jesus, it will be enough; but Jesus calls her out. Her answer to prayer is more than a healing; it is facing and overcoming her shame.

A Samaritan woman asks Jesus to explain to her where to worship. Jesus asks her about her husband, knowing full well she had none, but was living with a man. His answer to her shines a light on her brokenness. But it cuts to the last 10 percent. She leaves with living water.

A rich young man comes to Jesus hiding behind his goodness and his wealth. He dares Jesus to come up with something that he has missed in his righteousness. Jesus says, "Sell everything." In other words, you're holding back the last 10 percent of you—your wealth. Some theologians say that this man was the guy in Mark's Gospel who shows up in the garden of Gethsemane and runs away without his cloak. He had come to show Jesus that he had sold everything. And then theologians suspect this might be the writer of this Gospel . . . John Mark himself. Either way, Jesus's message is clear. *You're waiting on me? I'm waiting on your last 10 percent.*

> You're waiting on me? I'm waiting on your last 10 percent.

Could this have been what works in Zacchaeus's life as well? Here is this dirty, rotten scoundrel from all accounts: a Jewish man who turned on his people to work for the Romans and tax his own countrymen. He is so despised by everyone that he has to climb a tree just to watch Jesus walk by. Jesus won't leave him in his hiding; he calls him out and goes to his house for lunch. It's here that Zacchaeus shares the last 10 percent. "I've stolen. I'll give it back—interest."

Jesus knows what many of us take years to be convinced of: our secrets make us sick. Brené Brown in her TED talk says, "Put shame in a petri dish, and it needs three things to grow: secrecy, silence, judgment. Without these three realities, shame cannot survive." Jesus called people out into the light, where shame cannot live.

Come Clean

Max Lucado explains in his book *Anxious for Nothing* how specific prayer is helpful to relieve the burden of people's anxiety. When we come clean and get specific, it's as if we bring the huge, worrisome issue down to a manageable size.

Something magnificent seems to happen when we share the last 10 percent. It creates space for freedom. We take all the broken pieces of ourselves, and we drop them before our heavenly father and say, "I can't do this. Can you fix it?"

Not long after Sidney had "come clean" about the clothes, I had a chance to do the same. Our church had been trying to purchase land for years. Before I even got there, they thought they had a piece of property that would be perfect; but the city officials said, "Its not zoned for a church." This began a series of nos stretching into my tenure and lasting over several years. The process was getting quite familiar . . . we'd check on a piece of property; the city would tell us no. Repeat. Then one day, we found a building that had been recently vacated. We talked to the seller: he would sell to us. We had the down payment from the sale of our office building. We had a lender for the rest. And then we took it to the city. And you guessed it—they said, "It's not zoned for a church."

Let me pause right there. Because for the past six months, I had felt like my prayer times and journaling to God were getting more and more frustrated. I was getting into the last 10 percent. *God, isn't this what you wanted? Isn't the church your idea? Do you care about this as much as I do? Have you left us? You know this will only bring people to you!* I was getting good at being clear. This proved helpful.

So, when the city official said, "It's not zoned for a church," I was trained in sharing the last 10 percent. I said, "If not here . . . then where?" He was stunned. To be honest, so was I. I pushed my luck: "Every time we bring you something, you turn us down. I need a yes." He thought for a moment and then said, "Now that you mention it, there is a piece of property that has recently been rezoned. It could work for a church." I nearly passed out. He then went on to tell us the location. Then we all nearly passed out. It was the very first piece of property we had looked at three years prior. It was clear that it was the right place—just the wrong time.

Sharing the last 10 percent prepped me—and maybe even God—to say yes.

So, what's your last 10 percent with God?

God, I'm scared.

God, I'm hurt.

God, I'm anxious.

God, I'm hiding.

God, I'm alone.

God, I'm done.

While you wait, come out of the shadows, come clean, and share the last 10 percent.

He can take it.

Discussion Questions

1. When have you noticed someone telling you the last 10 percent?

2. Why do we struggle to speak the truth to God?

3. What is it that you want to say to God if you had the courage?

4. It's been said that anger is always the reaction to either fear or hurt. Which of these two causes the majority of your anger?

5. What is it time to tell God?

Next Steps

1. Make a list of what you're waiting on from God.

2. Now make a list of the last 10 percent of things you want to say.

Prayers as You Share the Last 10 Percent

"Lord, do not rebuke me in your anger or discipline me in your wrath. Have mercy on me, Lord, for I am faint; heal me, Lord, for my bones are in agony. My soul is in deep anguish. How long, Lord, how long? Turn, Lord, and deliver me; save me because of your unfailing love." (Ps. 6:1–4)

"When I kept silent, my bones wasted away through my groaning all day long. For day and night your hand was heavy on me; my strength was sapped as in the heat of summer. Then I acknowledged my sin to you and did not cover up my iniquity. I said, 'I will confess my transgressions to the Lord.' And you forgave the guilt of my sin." (Ps. 32:3–5)

"All my longings lie open before you, Lord; my sighing is not hidden from you. My heart pounds, my strength fails me; even the light has gone from my eyes. My friends and companions avoid me because of my wounds; my neighbors stay far away.... For I am about to fall, and my pain is ever with me. I confess my iniquity; I am troubled by my sin." (Ps. 38:9–11, 17–18)

"Have mercy on me, O God, according to your unfailing love; according to your great compassion blot out my transgressions. Wash away all my iniquity and cleanse me from my sin." (Ps. 51:1–2)

"Out of the depths I cry to you, Lord; Lord, hear my voice. Let your ears be attentive to my cry for mercy.

If you, LORD, kept a record of sins, LORD, who could stand? But with you there is forgiveness, so that we can, with reverence, serve you." (Ps. 130:1–4)

8

Run through the Checklist

I have two daughters. Which means there are three women living in my house. That means once a day, we run the risk of three hair dryers going at the same time. Three hair dryers, along with a couple of curling irons plugged in, and there's bound to be a phone charging, and all of this brings the real possibility that we will lose power. The struggle is real.

And when that moment happens, I hear the blow dryers all simultaneously cease, sometimes lights go dim, and I know the next word I will hear is a strong and panicked cry from one, if not all: "DAD!" That's my cue.

Let me make this clear: I am not an electrician, nor have I ever been mistaken for one. And while there are a few things

I can fix around the house, I tend to stay away from electricity. It can be dangerous. It's unforgiving. And, most importantly, I have no clue what I am doing. That being said, there are a couple of things I *can* check on.

First, the GFI switches. I have no idea what they are. For all I know, GFI might stand for "Go For It." But, I do know that they are on random outlets around the home. If there is a power surge, they can trip these switches and shut off power—not to the whole house, but to just a few outlets. So, I start walking around looking for all of these. It's a bit of an Easter egg hunt. When I find one, I press the button and hope that fixes the problem. But if it doesn't, I go to the next item on the checklist: the breaker box.

At our house, it's outside. This will require some shoes. Or at least slippers. I go outside, open the breaker box, and start looking. I guess what I'm hoping to see is a switch that has flashing green lights saying, "This is it!" But what I find is a bunch of switches that look the same. So I start flipping switches until I hear the blow dryers fire up again and the cries of merriment echo through the house all the way outside. If this doesn't work, I go to the next item on the checklist: call an electrician.

Most of us have a similar checklist when it comes to our prayer lives. When we sense God is not answering as quickly as we'd like, or when he's not giving us the answer we would like, we start to walk through a mental checklist of what we need to do to get God's attention:

Go to church?

Rosary beads?

Ask more people to pray?

Have a pastor vouch for you?

We all have a few things we think might help us flip the switch or make the connection work. We don't call them magic words, but we think that way.

In fact, it might be the reason you picked up this book. You were wondering if there were a few things you might be overlooking when it comes to getting what you want from God. I look for those things, too. What did I miss? What can I say? Is it a matter of lying on my face or praying just a little louder or longer?

While we've talked through many things we do while we wait on God's answer, the Bible does give us things we can stop doing to help reestablish a connection with God—a checklist, you might say. While these things don't make God love you any less, they are spoken of in Scripture as being things that keep us from having our prayers answered.

So, while you wait, here are a few things you might go over. These are seven biblical reasons why God doesn't answer our prayers as we request:

1. Unconfessed Sin

Sin is more than just a mistake or an accident; it is when we willfully decide that our choice is better than his command. It is when we are harboring a secret sin or practice that we know is outside God's intent, but we think if we just don't talk about it, it won't matter.

Here's a good way to know if you have unconfessed sin in your life: Is there anything that you are currently doing that if others found out, you'd be embarrassed? Is there anything you are trying to hide? Is there anything that makes you nervous that your spouse or your kids will discover? Is there anything you are currently doing that is hurtful to others? Anything in your life you are finding you have to justify or talk others into believing it's okay?

Look at how the prophet Isaiah addresses this in regard to the people of God: "Surely the arm of the LORD is not too short to save, nor his ear too dull to hear. But your iniquities have separated you from your God; your sins have hidden his face from you, so that he will not hear" (Isa. 59:1–2).

In other words, the issue is not his hearing or his power, but your sin. The issue of unconfessed sin is not about being perfect, but about being honest.

"I confess my lying."

"I'm coming clean on my prescription pills addiction."

"You're right. I'm selfish and self-consumed."

"This relationship has gone too far."

Is there anything you need to confess? Your unconfessed sin could be the reason you sense silence from God.

2. An Unforgiving Spirit

Isn't it easy to justify our lack of forgiveness toward other people, and yet demand forgiveness from others? We call it "being protective" or "just being honest," but most of the time, it's that we just don't want to forgive.

Think about how you feel when you scroll through social media. Are there certain people you see and inside you instinctively cringe? Maybe you've already blocked them or unfollowed them, but most of the time, we continue to cyber stalk them so we can see them face some difficulty in their life.

Ask yourself this: When others talk about that person posi-
tively, how long does it take for the "Yeah, buts" to begin in your
mind . . . and then exit your mouth?

"Yeah, but you don't know the whole story."

"Yeah, but if you ever worked with them, you'd feel differently."

"Yeah, but I could tell you another side."

Is there anyone you are holding a grudge against? Anyone
you are hoping will experience a fall from grace? Anyone you
are crossing your fingers to see trip on their shoestrings?

And let's be fair, you may even have good reason. They may
have done far worse to you than steal your lunch money or cut
you off in traffic, but the ramifications are the same. When we
hold a grudge, we hold up our own prayer life.

Jesus says this: "And when you stand praying, if you hold
anything against anyone, forgive him, so that your Father in
heaven may forgive you your sins" (Mark 11:25).

While you wait for your prayers to be answered, take some
time to pray for God's blessing on those on whom you'd rather
call down fire from heaven.

3. An Unbelieving Heart
We've covered this verse a few times:

> But when you ask, you must believe and not doubt,
> because the one who doubts is like a wave of the sea,
> blown and tossed by the wind. That person should
> not expect to receive anything from the Lord. Such a
> person is double-minded and unstable in all they do.
> (James 1:6–8)

James tells us that while perfect faith is not required, faith nonetheless is needed. Faith that the one you are talking to has the power to answer that prayer.

I think we all wonder if what we pray for is something that God *will* answer, but that's different than wondering if he *can* answer.

If people are not receiving what they expect to receive from God, Oswald Chambers writes that this is most likely because they are not adopting the right posture. He says, "Never say that it is not God's will to give you what you ask. Don't faint and give up, but find out the reason you have not received. . . . Have I been asking God to give me money for something I want, while refusing to pay someone what I owe him?"

In Chambers's view, people should not ask from a "desire for self-fulfillment," but rather from a pure heart and posture of a child. Chambers writes, "There is no use praying unless we are living as children of God. . . . Jesus says, regarding His children, 'Everyone who asks receives' (Matthew 7:8)."

I must confess that at times, I can put God in a box that limits my belief not in what he *has* done, but in what he *still* can do. Sure, he *can* heal, but will he? Sure, he *can* stop the storm, but will he? It's in these times of waiting that I need to pause and reflect on my level of faith.

So, do you believe that God is all-powerful, all-knowing, and able to do all things?

4. Improper Motives

This one is a little bit of a gut check. While God does want you to be honest and shoot straight, sometimes we ask with crossed fingers, thinking, *If I can just get this, it will solve all my problems.*

"When you ask, you do not receive, because you ask with wrong motives, that you may spend what you get on your pleasures" (James 4:3).

Prayers like this sound along the lines of "Can I get a date with her," or "If I can only win the lottery," or "God help me win this game and crush my opponent so that I am the object of everyone's praise!" (Okay, maybe we don't often say that one.) But many times my prayers are to limit my inconvenience or to help me save credibility. My motives are lacking when it comes to my asking.

> My motives are lacking when it comes to my asking.

A good way to test this is to ask, "If God says yes . . . does that make me look better or him look better?"

5. An Alienated Marriage Relationship

This is one we often overlook, but take a look at this passage we read from Peter: "Husbands, in the same way be considerate as you live with your wives, and treat them with respect as the weaker partner and as heirs with you of the gracious gift of life, so that nothing will hinder your prayers" (1 Pet. 3:7).

While there is so much to unpack in this verse, the main point is that how we treat our spouse can impact how God hears our prayers. Back to Jesus's one commandment he gave us: to love others the way he has loved us! So if we are not doing that in our home, it can impact how we connect with him.

I think about this as a pastor. I have the responsibility to stand on stage and pray for people and ask God to bless them and his church. But, I do so also hoping that my wife who is in the congregation isn't thinking, *What a hypocrite!* I don't want to be one way at church and another at home.

Or as the old pastor joke goes: The pastor's wife said to her husband, "How about this Sunday you do something different. You be grumpy at church and charming at home."

Peter is saying here that your honesty and humility impacts your prayers. If we want the joy of seeing and savoring God in Christ, we must not make peace with our sins. We must make war. The almost incredible hope of confessing and renouncing sin is that the Lord does not then rub it in our face, but cancels it.

6. An Anemic Effort

There is something to be said about passionate prayers.

> So Peter was kept in prison, but the church was earnestly praying to God for him. (Acts 12:5)

> Elijah was a human being, even as we are. He prayed earnestly that it would not rain, and it did not rain on the land for three and a half years. (James 5:17)

I know this with my kids around Christmastime. If while my daughter and I are watching TV a commercial comes on for a new piece of technology and she says, "I'd like that for Christmas," I immediately file it away. But, if she never brings it up again, or moves on to other things, I just let it go. She probably didn't really need or even want the thing that we saw on TV. But if she tells me a story about how that device can greatly change her life, I lean in. If she sends me several links through texts for the next few weeks, I get the point. She really wants this.

We've looked at several stories of persistent widows and fathers begging for help for their families. Jesus tells us these are circumstances that cause our heavenly Father to lean in.

7. The Sovereignty of God

"'I will have mercy on whom I have mercy, and I will have compassion on whom I have compassion.' It does not, therefore, depend on human desire or effort, but on God's mercy" (Rom. 9:15–16).

At the end of the day, God is in charge.

These principles are on my mind because of the recent death of a woman in our church. Thousands of Christians prayed for her to be healed of cancer. They not only prayed, they fasted and prayed. The elders anointed her with oil and prayed.

While she lived two years longer than doctors had projected, her condition continued to deteriorate, and she died at age forty-eight. Those seemingly unanswered prayers left many perplexed as to why God doesn't always answer such intensified prayers affirmatively.

Considering the number of righteous people who prayed with intensity and with pure motives for her to recover, I can only conclude our prayers were not answered simply because it was not in the will of God. That doesn't make sense to us, but God's ways are not our ways.

Job challenged God's fairness and asked why so many horrible things were happening to him when he had lived a righteous life. God finally responded by asking Job where he was when the world was created. Could he explain the formation of a baby in the womb or summon the lightning to appear in the sky? God didn't give any clear answers as to why Job was hurting so much. He just reminded Job that he was God and that Job should trust him to work things out in the end.

Philip Yancey, in his classic work *Disappointment with God*, heavily encourages people to adopt God's perspective, instead of relying on a limited human perspective. People ask questions about God's reasoning and actions, and Yancey even expresses his own frustrations: "But even as I pray, I wonder. Can God be trusted? If so many small prayers go unanswered, what about the big ones?"

Yancey responds to these frustrations with a shift in perspective, and explains, "God lives on a 'higher' level, in another dimension. The universe does not contain him; he created the universe." Yancey hopes for people to understand that they are not even able to comprehend God's power and wisdom; and in order to prove this point, he rephrases a conversation between Job and God. Yancey writes,

> "Why are you treating me so unfairly, God?" Job has whined throughout the book. "Put yourself in my place."
>
> "NO!!!" God thunders in reply. "You put yourself in *my* place! Until you can offer lessons on how to make the sun come up each day . . . don't judge how I run the world. Just shut up and listen."

Yancey explains that because of this conversation between God and Job, "God had given Job a glimpse of the big picture." If people can understand that they are incapable of understanding God's master plan for their lives, but can trust in God's infinite power and wisdom, then Yancey believes that their lives *after* prayer will be improved. He finishes the argument by talking about the limited human perspective, and says, "By no means can we infer that our own trials are, like Job's, specially arranged by God to settle some decisive issue in the universe. But we can safely assume that our limited range of vision will in similar fashion distort reality."

God doesn't promise that all our prayers will be answered just as we express them. He does promise that he hears our prayers and, in the end, all will be made right. In the meantime, ours is not to understand or explain but to trust and to wait.

So, why would God say yes to some and no to others? That's what we'll talk about next.

Discussion Questions

1. What's your checklist that you use around the house most?

2. What do you tend to do when you think your prayers aren't being answered?

3. Which of these seven reasons God might not be answering your prayers is the easiest to overlook?

4. Which of these seven reasons is the toughest to resolve?

5. In whom can you confide about these?

Next Steps

1. Go through the checklist.

2. Make things right.

Prayers as You Run through the Checklist

"Look on me and answer, Lord my God. Give light to my eyes, or I will sleep in death . . . I trust in your unfailing love; my heart rejoices in your salvation. I will sing the Lord's praise, for he has been good to me." (Ps. 13:3, 5–6)

"When my prayers returned to me unanswered, I went about mourning as though for my friend or brother. . . . Lord, you have seen this; do not be silent. Do not be far from me, Lord. Awake, and rise to my defense! Contend for me, my God and Lord." (Ps. 35:13–14, 22–23)

"We are given no signs from God; no prophets are left, and none of us knows how long this will be. How long will the enemy mock you, God? Will the foe revile your name forever? Why do you hold back your hand, your right hand?" (Ps. 74:9–11)

"Do not hold against us the sins of past generations; may your mercy come quickly to meet us, for we are in desperate need. Help us, God our Savior, for the glory of your name; deliver us and forgive our sins for your name's sake." (Ps. 79:8–9)

"Teach me your way, Lord, that I may rely on your faithfulness; give me an undivided heart, that I may fear your name. I will praise you, Lord my God, with all my heart; I will glorify your name forever. For great is your love toward me; you have delivered me from the depths, from the realm of the dead." (Ps. 86:11–13)

9

Prepare along the Way

"I'm ready when you are."

These are words that every husband has said to his wife. Getting ready to go for my wife takes exactly one hour (add possibly an additional fifteen minutes). It's a little like watching a soccer match. You don't know when the game will be over, the clock is irrelevant; you are just guessing. So, I prepare to be ready when she is ready. I go downstairs. I get my keys. I might even start the car. I've learned that honking the horn is never a good idea. I go ahead and get her purse, get her a water bottle (as one is always needed when we leave home). But I do everything in my power to be absolutely prepared for when she walks down the stairs and says, "Let's go . . . I'm ready."

During this time, I wait for a signal—a sign that says she's truly ready. The sign is not her saying, "I'm almost ready!" The sign is not even, "Get the car started." The sign is one sound: the sound of hair spray. Even the dogs know that sound as a sign she is headed down the stairs. They run the stairs and wait for her arrival, which may mean a treat. Hair spray is the sound of "I'm finished prepping; now I'm ready."

Praying feels a lot like waiting for the sound of hair spray. I'm pretty sure that sentence has never been written until now.

Like most, I keep a prayer list. It's not fancy, but it's a list of names and ideas and hopes and dreams that I bring to God often. Like I told you before, I used to keep it in a journal, then a calendar, but now I keep it on my Notes app on my phone. This is helpful so I can look at it periodically throughout the day and so I can add to it easily when someone tells me something that needs to go on the list.

There are names of family members whom I pray for God to protect and keep safe. There are names of church members who have upcoming medical procedures, tests, court appearances, job interviews, struggling marriages, wayward kids, and more. These requests all seem to fall under the prayer of "God, they need you to be near . . . and when you are near, would you help them in any way they need?"

Then there is the list of hopes and dreams.

"God, will you help my kids get into college?" The prayer is always followed with "God, will you help us be able to pay for college?"

"Father, will you bring us the right staff member to fill this open role?"

"God, will you soften the hearts of my neighbors so they might come to church?"

You have a list as well. You may write it down, you may just keep it in the forefront of your mind, but you've got a list.

"God, help my cancer not to return."

"God, please lead me to the right spouse."

"God, I pray for a job."

"God, will you help my kids come back to you?"

"God, will you make it clear how to care for my aging parents?"

These are all prayers of supernatural wisdom or intervention. "God, I don't know what to do . . . God, I'm in over my head here . . . God, I need you to do something big here."

And then we wait. And we hope for the best. We hope to hear hair spray.

The first church in the first century dealt with this. Some of these people had seen Jesus. Some were friends with people that he had healed. Can you imagine sitting in church with the former blind man whom Jesus healed? Every time you would look him in the eyes, you would be reminded that miracles happen. Furthermore, this church had direct access to the apostle Peter: the guy who had the greatest comeback of all time, from denying Jesus to launching the church at Pentecost. People are even being healed by his shadow casting on them. What an incredible time to be the church!

However, it's also a difficult time to be the church. They are smashed between two opposing forces: the empire of Rome and the temple. The Jewish community wants them gone. The political and governmental community wants them gone. And it seems like the leaders of the faith keep getting arrested. The questions over coffee and donuts at church would be different than ours. Questions like: "So, was Jesus speaking hypothetically when he said, 'The gates of hell will not prevail'? Didn't Jesus say, 'I will be with you always'? Surely things should be a bit easier than this."

That's when we find the first church at an all-night prayer vigil. In the book of Acts, we read that Peter had been arrested and so the church gathered together for prayer. I'm sure some people brought some food, others brought in some folding chairs and put on a pot of coffee—all things needed for an all-night prayer meeting. Maybe someone sang a song and then they took time to go around the circle for prayer requests. "Harvest is coming." "Billy got suspended from school." "Unspoken." There's often the prayer request that borders on gossip: "We need to pray for Helen; she found lipstick on her husband's collar."

Maybe their prayer vigil didn't look at all like ours . . . but they still gathered to pray. And they were praying for Peter's release.

Somewhere between the prayer requests and the coffee break, while everyone was praying for Peter to be set free, they hear a knock at the door. We read that a young woman named Rhoda is sent to answer it while everyone continues to beg God for Peter's release. She says, "Who is it?" The voice on the other side says, "It's Peter."

She goes back to the group and declares, "It's Peter!" To which they say, "It can't be—he's in prison. Let's keep praying for his release." I'm not sure how many times Peter had to knock, but finally, someone let him in and they were all completely shocked. And to be honest, I would have been too.

In the early days of our church, we met in a movie theater on Sunday mornings. It wasn't ideal, but it was all we could do at the time. We were hoping to one day buy land and build a building, but it was tricky because we were a new church and land is so expensive in California. The one thing we did have was an old funeral home that we purchased on the cheap. It had a small chapel, big enough for a leader gathering or small Bible study, but not nearly big enough for Sunday morning service. Yet it did have some office space that was adequate for our staff. So, when a piece of property came up that might work for us, we gathered our elders together in a room in our makeshift office building and said, "How can we possibly find a way to buy this?" One of our elders said, "What if we sold this building and used the money for a down payment on the land?" I said, "That's a great idea! But who would want this place? How can we possibly find a buyer for this?" That's when a CPA in our group—a guy who you'd think would only be thinking about numbers—said something more spiritual than I, the pastor: "Why don't we pray about it?" Uh, yeah . . . I was going to say that.

So we prayed. We prayed and asked if God would send us a buyer for this building if he wanted us to buy land. And I kid you not, fifteen minutes later, while we were still having our meeting, two gentlemen came into the office, were greeted by the receptionist, and they said, "We are from a new church looking for a building. This site would be perfect for us. Have you ever considered selling it?" When our receptionist came in and relayed the message, we were all stunned. I'm embarrassed to say that I was not the one to suggest we pray. And I'm even more embarrassed to say that my first reaction was not, "Praise God! Just as I believed he would!" But rather, "Are you kidding me?" I get Rhoda. I am Rhoda.

Months after this, I was lamenting my shock at God answering our prayers to sell the building, when one of our elders said to me, "You do realize we've all been praying and planning for this moment for some time." He was right, and suddenly I felt better.

For the previous three years, we had been looking at and praying for land, marching around buildings, and asking God to do something big. This moment of the knock on the door was not the beginning of the story, but about twenty chapters in.

So, what do we do while we wait for chapter twenty?

Start Walking in the Right Direction

Much like when Mary came to Jesus and asked him to turn water into wine, we need to learn to prepare for the miracle before it happens. When Mary approached Jesus, he answered her with a statement that seemed to imply that he was not going to grant her request. However, she began to prepare as though the miracle was already on its way. She started getting the servants ready to "do whatever he says." Sometimes there are preparations to be made while we wait for his answer.

> We need to learn to prepare for the miracle before it happens.

In Luke's account of Jesus, we read about a time Jesus is approached by ten lepers. No, that's not ten cats. Nor is it victims of Hansen's disease. These are people with a skin condition that is so vile they are forced to live in leper colonies away from their family and friends. There is no cure. They are forced to shout, "Unclean," if anyone comes near them. To make matters worse, this disease was generally associated with sin in a person's life. We also learn that these ten are not all Jewish. One is Samaritan, which shows us how devastating this disease is because they only have each other. Normally these two backgrounds would never associate with each other, but struggle tends to make the most unlikely of friends.

Jesus had been approached by lepers before. More than likely, word had gotten out that Jesus was able to heal this disease. And in those cases, Jesus touched them and they were healed immediately. These lepers were hoping Jesus would touch them and heal them in an instant.

However, in this case, Jesus takes a different approach:

> He looked at them and said, "Go show yourselves to the priests." And as they went, they were cleansed of their leprosy.
>
> One of them, when he saw that he was healed, came back to Jesus, shouting, "Praise God!" He fell to the ground at Jesus' feet, thanking him for what he had done. This man was a Samaritan.
>
> Jesus asked, "Didn't I heal ten men? Where are the other nine? Has no one returned to give glory to God except this foreigner?" And Jesus said to the man, "Stand up and go. Your faith has healed you." (Luke 17:14–19 NLT)

Jesus doesn't touch them and give them immediate healing. Instead, Jesus orders them to do some work. No quick fix here, but rather a "Go and show the priest." Why?

They knew that this was the law for ceremonial cleansing. If they were healed, before they could return to their families, they had to get it signed off on by a priest. But since they were not healed just yet, this would have been rather presumptuous on their part. They'd have to make the journey to find a priest, they'd have to be around others, and all while assuming they were actually going to be healed at some point.

And somewhere along their journey, that's exactly what happened. Why does Jesus say yes to their prayer this way?

Maybe it's to show us that there is no one-size-fits-all answer. No magic words or formula. One person is touched; others have to trust as they go.

Maybe it's to see whom they consider their priest. The nine Jews go and find a priest. But the Samaritan has no priest to go to . . . so he comes back to Jesus.

Whatever it may be, here's what we do know: something was required *of* them before healing happened *to* them. Jesus gave them a command, and they had to act. Their healing happened on the way.

I wonder how long it took. Did they walk for miles and question what they were doing? Did two of them say, "This is stupid," while the other eight talked them into keeping going?

People like to wonder if the nine who didn't return to say thank you got their leprosy back. There is no mention of that. It seems that the miracle was not contingent on the "thank you," but rather on the "trust me." Go; show yourself to the priest. Trust me.

How natural does it come for you to prepare for God's answer along the way? When my prayers seem to be unanswered, I wonder if I didn't trust enough. Yet, there is no evidence that these men saw Jesus as anything more than a rabbi with a magic touch. There is no promise of faith.

> Something was required *of* them before healing happened *to* them.

There is no declaration of "I'll follow wherever you lead." Just a request from them and a command from him.

Noticing God's Answers

Henry Blackaby says this about what happens after we pray and start preparing along the way: "You pray in agreement with the will of God. You adjust your thinking and attitudes to God's truth. You look and listen for confirmation or further direction from the Bible, circumstances, and the church (other believers). Finally, you obey."

Maybe the preparing along the way is what helps me notice God's answer. I've noticed a big difference in how I feel about my prayer life when one thing is involved: writing it down. Much like how people claim to lose weight when they simply start writing down what they eat. They begin to think about what it is they are consuming throughout the day, and suddenly they are more cognizant of their daily calorie intake. When I write down my prayers, I'm more likely to notice when they are answered. I begin looking for what to record next, which makes me more likely to see what God might be doing. It also forces me to keep doing the last thing God told me to do, until the next thing comes along. Simply writing it down keeps me focused on what God might do, while I continue to finish what he last told me to do.

What is it you have to "do along the way"?

Maybe your prayer is about a physical healing. You've asked God for healing . . . but you keep going to the doctor, taking your medications, and fighting. You never know how God might use these things to bring about your healing.

Maybe your prayer is about a career promotion. You've asked God for an opportunity, but you find you are just waiting around for someone to come and find you. DeVon Franklin, a movie producer whose credits include *Breakthrough* and *Heaven Is for Real*, recommends working on your craft while you wait. "What if your prayers for career advancement have already been answered, but they have not manifested because you aren't displaying the discipline required to handle the opportunity?" Maybe you need to find a mentor, chase down every opportunity, and work to become the person you would hire while you wait for someone else to see this in you as well.

Maybe your prayer is about a relationship. You ask God to heal your marriage, but you feel you are the only one interested in making it better. Maybe you need to own your part, work on your communication skills, read marriage books, plan weekend getaways, and become an expert in your spouse's personality and love language.

Maybe your prayer is about your own soul. You ask God for joy, for peace, for contentment, but you're restless, depressed, and anxious. You still do what is best; you do your part . . . until you are healed along the way. It is during this time of prayer and waiting that God begins to shift our plans to his plans, our perspective to his perspective, and our will to his will.

Corrie ten Boom knew something about waiting on God. She waited for years in a concentration camp during World War II. Night after night, she would pray for her release, the end of the war, and the reunion of her family. She writes this about God's seeming silence: "We never know how God will answer our prayers, but we can expect that He will get us involved in His plan for the answer. If we are true intercessors, we must be ready to take part in God's work on behalf of the people for whom we pray."

I once had an intern working for me who was praying for a ministry position, a healthy life, and a thriving relationship that would lead to marriage and kids. The problem was he was struggling with depression. His mom had died of cancer, his father was out of the picture, and he was a philosophy major with more on his mind than he could process. His prayers were consistent and not out of the scope of what God might say yes to. He was like the leper who approached Jesus. He wasn't asking to win the lottery or be given a new Porsche. He was begging for life, community, and wholeness. So as he prayed . . . he went to a doctor. The doctor gave him a prescription to help with his depression, but he then said, "There are many slices to the pie when it comes to healing. You don't just take meds and hope for the best. You need to sleep eight hours a night. You need to eat healthy. You need to exercise daily. And you need to pursue healthy relationships." Sounds a lot like "Go show yourself to the priest." Start walking in the right direction, make the right choices, prepare along the way, and you will walk yourself into a blessing.

And that's what he did. He now leads a powerful campus ministry for thousands of college students. He has a thriving marriage, three beautiful children, and leads a large staff of interns just like he once was. And occasionally, he has to tell them the story of how he walked his way into healing.

Discussion Questions

1. If you were one of the ten lepers, would it have been easy to start heading toward the priest even though you weren't healed yet?

2. What are you currently praying for that is taking forever?

3. What might God be telling you to do as you prepare along the way?

4. Is there anyone you know of who is currently preparing along the way?

5. How can you help them as they wait?

Next Steps

1. Take time to send an encouraging text to someone who you know is waiting for an answer from God.

2. Update your prayer list with any answers you have seen from God.

Prayers as You Prepare along the Way

"I remain confident of this: I will see the goodness of the LORD in the land of the living. Wait for the LORD; be strong and take heart and wait for the LORD." (Ps. 27:13–14)

"Be still before the LORD and wait patiently for him." (Ps. 37:7)

"He says, 'Be still, and know that I am God; I will be exalted among the nations, I will be exalted in the earth.' The LORD Almighty is with us; the God of Jacob is our fortress." (Ps. 46:10–11)

"Out of the depths I cry to you, LORD; Lord, hear my voice. Let your ears be attentive to my cry for mercy." (Ps. 130:1–2)

"I wait for the LORD, my whole being waits, and in his word I put my hope. I wait for the Lord more than watchmen wait for the morning, more than watchmen wait for the morning." (Ps. 130:5–6)

10

Remember

When I was nineteen years old, I was diagnosed with diabetes.

There are two types of diabetes: Type 1 is the kind that requires taking daily injections of insulin. Type 2 requires taking a pill. I have type 1. Yep, the kid who was terrified of going to the doctor for fear of getting a shot is now forced to take up to four injections a day. Needless to say, I wasn't thrilled by this news.

Over the next five years, I learned to deal with this new norm in my life. I had settled into a rhythm that worked for me, and I was getting used to it. That is until I met a man in our church who came up to me and said, "I'm going to begin praying for your healing from this disease." My first thought was, "Oh, that's kind. But I'll manage." But then I thought, well, why not? He encouraged me to pray for this healing as well. So, I did. And over the next few months and years, it became clear that God said no to this prayer.

During this time, we had a tragedy in our church. A nineteen-year-old student had a car accident that left her fighting for her life. She was in the ICU for weeks while the church rallied and prayed for God's healing and full recovery for this young woman with her future ahead of her. How could this be a bad thing? Wouldn't this be restoring her to community? Wouldn't this bring God glory? God spared her life but did not grant her a full recovery. It is clear in this situation that God's answer to our prayers for healing was, "Yes, but not in the way you had hoped."

A few years after this, some dear friends of ours had a series of miscarriages. This was a wonderful couple with a warm and inviting home prepared to raise children to honor God. Why would God deny them this opportunity? I remember during this time hearing a story of a pregnant teen who, unbeknownst to everyone, while at her high school prom, delivered her baby in the school bathroom and went back to the dance. The child died. I couldn't even begin to make sense of this. Why would God deny my friends a pregnancy, yet allow one for this girl who clearly was not ready to be a parent?

I could go on and on. And so could you, I'm sure of it. So far, we have talked about six things to do while you wait:

1. Align with the "Why"
2. Yield the "How"
3. Do the Next Right Thing

4. Share the Last 10 Percent
5. Run through the Checklist
6. Prepare along the Way

But, let's say that you've done these six things. You've aligned with the "why," you've even given up the "how," you've shared the last 10 percent, you've gone over the checklist, you are in the process of doing the next right thing, and you are preparing for the miracle as you go—but the longer you wait, you are discovering that the answer you are looking for may not be a yes . . . or a wait . . . but possibly a no.

Responses to No

Since Jesus is not a magic wand or genie, but rather God with a plan, we sometimes don't get exactly what we ask for. So, how do we live with that? How do we find the faith to pray again? What do we do when the waiting on God is turning into a no from God? Here's what we tend to do:

Throw a Fit

Sounds childish, doesn't it? We've seen our kids do this. We've seen other people's kids do this.

It reminds me of the story of a man pushing his young son in a grocery cart through a store. Every aisle they went down led to more demands from the boy. Every time the father said no or tried to redirect the child's attention, the son would throw a fit. Screaming, crying, lashing out. Quietly, the father would whisper, "It's okay, Patrick. We're almost done." This happened multiple times. And every time, the father would say, "It's okay, Patrick. We're almost done." Finally, when they were heading out of the store, another customer who had witnessed all of this took a moment to encourage the father: "I just wanted to say I admire how patient you were with your son Patrick." The exhausted father looked at the customer and said, "Oh, his name isn't Patrick—mine is!"

Ever thrown a fit with God? I have. Begging, pleading, threatening. Listing off all that we've done right and all that we haven't done wrong. I've been known to throw others under the bus in my fit throwing with God. "Look how much better I am than they are!" "Why do you seem to answer their prayers and not mine?"

The silence I hear often spirals me downward. "How dare you. You know this would be good. I can't believe you would do this. How can this prayer be bad or selfish? It's for your glory." Other than getting some stuff off my chest, this type of reaction to God's silence doesn't really help me.

Blame

A close second to my fit throwing is my tendency to blame.

Sometimes, we blame ourselves: "I messed this up." "It's all my fault." "I must have done something wrong." We go over the checklist time and time again. Did I miss something?

Sometimes, we blame others: "I have faith, but you must not." "It's all your fault." "I'm the only one pulling the spiritual weight in this home!" We tend to think that if only our families would pray more, or go to church with us, or get their acts together, then God would answer *our* prayers.

But mostly, we blame God: "How could you do this?" It causes us to question the very nature of God.

The writers of Psalms did their share of this:

Will you be angry with us always?
>Will you prolong your wrath to all generations?
Won't you revive us again,
>so your people can rejoice in you?
Show us your unfailing love, O LORD,
>and grant us your salvation. (Ps. 85:5–7 NLT)

O LORD, how long will this go on?
>Will you hide yourself forever?
>How long will your anger burn like fire?
Remember how short my life is,
>how empty and futile this human existence!
No one can live forever; all will die.
>No one can escape the power of the grave.
Lord, where is your unfailing love?
>You promised it to David with a faithful pledge.
Consider, Lord, how your servants are disgraced!
>I carry in my heart the insults of so many people.
Your enemies have mocked me, O LORD;
>they mock your anointed king wherever he goes.
>(Ps. 89:46–51 NLT)

Where is God when I wait . . . and where is God when I get a no? David will write other psalms about waiting, and it's interesting that he often follows up "wait" with the word "hope":

We wait in hope for the LORD;
>he is our help and our shield.
In him our hearts rejoice,
>for we trust in his holy name.
May your unfailing love be with us, LORD,

even as we put our hope in you. (Ps. 33:20–22)

Wait and hope for and expect the Lord; be brave and of good courage and let your heart be stout and enduring. Yes, wait for and hope for and expect the Lord. (Ps. 27:14 AMPC)

I wait for the Lord
    more than watchmen wait for the morning,
    more than watchmen wait for the morning.
    (Ps. 130:6)

Actually, the word "wait" here means, "hopeful expectation." While he may not have hope that he'll get what he wants, he still does not lose hope. This is a bit like waiting for a friend at the airport. You drive there; you circle the airport, waiting on the text saying, "we've landed"; but you hear nothing. Eventually, you park and go inside. You see on the board that the flight is delayed but on its way. So you wait. You have not lost hope.

Now, let's say they reroute your friend to another airport due to some bad weather where you are. Now you have to wait another day. Or, let's say they show up by taxi, or by you going to get them. You still have hope that you will see them.

You are turning "hopeless waiting" into "waiting hopefully."

In *Disappointment with God*, Philip Yancey says that he wrote the book because "I found that for many people there is a large gap between what they *expect* from their Christian faith and what they actually experience" (emphasis mine). By using the two tactics I mentioned above, Yancey hopes to support people in their frustrations *after* prayer. In short, we lack the hope when we wait.

He goes on to give reasons why God might not be responding to prayers in the ways people expect. He references the miracle of transfiguration, which involved Peter, James, and John, and describes how these disciples lost faith shortly after the event. Yancey writes, "Yet what effect did this stupendous event have on Jesus' three closest friends, Peter, James, and John? Did it permanently silence their questions and fill them with faith? A few weeks later, when Jesus needed them the most, they all forsook him."

Yancey hypothesizes that even when people experience miraculous displays of God's power and wisdom, they still might not trust in God more or, more importantly, love God more. Yancey believes that in God's perspective, miraculous responses to prayer are not his first priority. Yancey writes, "He created us to love him, but his most impressive displays of miracle—the kind we may secretly long for—do nothing to foster that love." Furthermore, Yancey writes, "God freely admits he is holding back his power, but he restrains himself for our benefit." Let me give you a third option. And this is our seventh thing to do while waiting on God.

Remember

Occasionally, I will say something I regret (I say "occasionally," my wife says "often"). But once in a while, I will make an insensitive comment to my wife. It's not intentional; it's not out of anger or bitterness; it's really just me being a guy. Sometimes I forget I'm not living in the college dorm with a bunch of guys who constantly rip each other. So when I say something that I think is funny, and she is not laughing, it is clear that I have overstepped. She'll give me the look, or speak words of correction, or sometimes I'll figure it out first and apologize, and then she has a choice. Will she choose to believe this is who I am . . . or will she remember who I've been?

While God doesn't slip up and say something sarcastic to us, we do have to ask, "When I don't get the answer I want . . . will I change my perspective on who God is? Or will I remember who God has been?"

The Israelites had to make a practice of this. For much of their existence, the stories of creation, the flood, Abraham, and God's presence were stories they had to continually tell each other.

While they were enslaved for decades, they had to remind each other . . . we serve the God who promised Father Abraham we would be a great nation.

While they wandered in the wilderness, they had to remind each other . . . we serve a God who rescued Isaac; he can surely rescue us.

While they waited in exile to Babylon, they had to remind each other . . . we serve a God who delivered our forefathers; he will deliver us.

This is tough for us to do at times, because we tend to hold God to things he hasn't promised. Kate Bowler had to wrestle with this when as a young mom she was diagnosed with cancer. In her book *Everything Happens for a Reason . . . and Other Lies I've Loved*, she tackles the disappointment we feel with God when he says no. According to Kate, the gospel says God will make you rich and whole, but this does not always mean you will be wealthy and healed.

We must remember that the gospel we follow has a leader who said, "In this world you will have trouble. But take heart! I have overcome the world" (John 16:33).

We must remember that the gospel we claim is one of eternal restoration, not momentary pleasure.

We must remember that if our leader died on a cross, then our standard of blessing can't be a life without pain.

Max Lucado, in his book *Anxious for Nothing,* builds his premise off this one verse: "Be anxious for nothing, but in everything by prayer and supplication, with thanksgiving, let your requests be made known to God; and the peace of God, which surpasses all understanding, will guard your hearts and minds through Christ Jesus" (Phil. 4:6–7 NKJV).

Alluding to this verse, Lucado talks about the joy of trusting in God's sovereignty. He says, "Rather than rehearse the chaos of the world, rejoice in the Lord's sovereignty, as Paul did." Lucado is passionate about this idea of trusting in God's sovereignty, and even goes on to say, "Is God sovereign over your circumstances? Is he mightier than your problem? Does he have answers to your questions? According to the Bible the answer is yes, yes, and yes!"

Sometimes in my prayers, I blame God for the lack of things that he *has not* promised, rather than remembering his provision of what he *has.*

The apostle Paul came to understand this. We touched on this briefly in a previous chapter, but let's dig into the complexity of it now.

Paul had limited knowledge of Jesus from where he was in Tarsus. All he knew was that this guy was stirring up trouble for his beloved Jews. So after he heard Jesus had died, he went to stamp out all Jesus's followers. On his trip to Damascus, his journey ended with him meeting Jesus face to face and being given a new calling: to tell others about him.

Over the next two years, Paul learned the stories of Jesus from the disciples and the first church members who had seen it all with their own eyes. Then, silence. He went home. He made tents. And he waited. He told people back in Tarsus about Jesus, but no one seemed to care. His family thought he was crazy. But he kept talking . . . and waiting. Is this really the call Jesus had for him? But he remembered what the disciples told him about Jesus. *He can be trusted. Just wait.* And ten years later Barnabus knocked on his door and said, "It's time."

For the next thirteen years, he travels, teaches, is in and out of prison, is left for dead, plants churches, mentors young pastors, and is finally seeing the fruit of his calling. But in 2 Corinthians we read this journey has not been without its difficulty. Paul writes that he dealt with a "thorn in his side"—a "messenger of Satan." Scholars like to debate what this might have been—perhaps failing eyesight, perhaps malaria. But here's what we do know . . . Paul begged the Lord to take it away:

> Three different times I begged the Lord to take it
> away. Each time he said, "My grace is all you need.
> My power works best in weakness." So now I am
> glad to boast about my weaknesses, so that the
> power of Christ can work through me. That's why I
> take pleasure in my weaknesses, and in the insults,
> hardships, persecutions, and troubles that I suffer

for Christ. For when I am weak, then I am strong. (2 Cor. 12:8–10 NLT)

This affliction didn't come at the end of years of success; it came at the beginning. Before he even began his missionary trips. But what did Paul do? He remembered what the disciples had told him about Jesus. Surely they mentioned on the night before he was crucified he said, "In this world you will have trouble. But take heart! I have overcome the world" (John 16:33). So Paul waited . . . with hope.

John knew this.

John was an eyewitness to all Jesus did. And he was Jesus's closest friend. You'd think that would garner some favor from Jesus after he had returned to heaven, but John still had his wandering and wondering.

Soon after the church begins, they experience signs, wonders, and rapid growth. Until persecution breaks out. John's brother James is executed. How could this be? He was also a disciple, a close friend of Jesus. And John has to wonder, *Why him and not me?* He must have remembered when Jesus said, "In this world you will have trouble. But take heart! I have overcome the world."

Over the next decade, John would see mass persecution take the lives of friends, church members, and even the other disciples. He himself would be tortured and left on a prison island to die. He must have remembered "In this world you will have trouble . . ." But he also must have found it hard to "take heart."

So, Jesus showed up. The book the Revelation is the letter John writes to his persecuted churches from the vision he received from Jesus. And you know what Jesus told him?

> I heard a loud shout from the throne, saying, "Look, God's home is now among his people! He will live with them, and they will be his people. God himself will be with them. He will wipe every tear from their eyes, and there will be no more death or sorrow or crying or pain. All these things are gone forever." (Rev. 21:3–4 NLT)

Remember. I have overcome the world. I may not take away the pain, but one day I'll take away the tears.

Teresa of Avila goes so far as to say we are simply unable to know what is best for us. Presuming we do and then asking God to fix things our way is a bit shortsighted of us. She suggests we simply keep praying until our will conforms to his. There is power found in being specific, even if we get it wrong. God has a way of using our clumsy prayers to perfect our faith.

My friends who suffered multiple miscarriages scoffed at the phrase people would say to try to comfort them: "Everything happens for a reason." But my friend had a great response he learned while waiting on God, searching the Scriptures, and remembering the character of Christ. And I think this is what John and Paul and all the saints before us have discovered and now know in glory.

The truth is not "everything happens for a reason," but rather "everything can be redeemed." And one day, the crucified Lord will wipe every tear from our eyes and all will be made right.

Remember this.

Discussion Questions

1. What are you waiting on from God?

2. Are you dealing with a "thorn in your side?"

3. Are you more likely to assume God has forgotten you or do you assume he has another plan for you?

4. What story or quality about God do you need to remember?

5. What do you need to see God redeem?

Next Steps

1. Read through the Gospels and make a list of all the things Jesus did for people.

2. Turn these into a "remember the time" list to be reflected upon often.

Prayers When You Hear No

"How long, LORD? Will you forget me forever? How long will you hide your face from me? How long must I wrestle with my thoughts and day after day have sorrow in my heart?" (Ps. 13:1–2)

"Look on me and answer, LORD my God. Give light to my eyes . . . . I trust in your unfailing love; my heart rejoices in your salvation. I will sing the LORD's praise, for he has been good to me." (Ps. 13:3, 5–6)

"I remembered you, God, and I groaned; I meditated, and my spirit grew faint. You kept my eyes from closing; I was too troubled to speak. . . . 'Will the Lord reject forever? Will he never show his favor again? Has his unfailing love vanished forever? Has his promise failed for all time? Has God forgotten to be merciful? Has he in anger withheld his compassion?'" (Ps. 77:3–4, 7–9)

"'I will remember the deeds of the LORD; yes, I will remember your miracles of long ago. I will consider all your works and meditate on all your mighty deeds.' Your ways, God, are holy. What god is as great as our God? You are the God who performs miracles; you display your power among the peoples." (Ps. 77:11–14)

"Your word, LORD, is eternal; it stands firm in the heavens. Your faithfulness continues through all generations; you established the earth, and it endures. Your laws endure to this day, for all things serve you. If your law had not been my delight, I would have perished in my affliction. I will never forget your precepts, for by them you have preserved my life." (Ps. 119:89–93)

11

Why Bother?

By now you've figured out that I have a wait problem. And by that, I mean an "I hate to wait" problem. I don't think I'm alone in this. Unfortunately, there are not groups like Wait Watchers or Wait Down groups; there are just those of us who are impatient and sighing and looking at our watches.

One time while rushing through an airport, I did what seemed like a logical thing to do when you have a wait problem: I needed to get to my gate, but I also needed Starbucks. As always, the line for Starbucks was a mile long; and though I probably could have waited in it and still made my plane, I hate to wait. So, I walked to the front of the line where a man was about to order and said, "I'll give you $10 to order me a medium-sized black coffee." He was surprised—probably a bit startled that some stranger had just invaded his space, but he agreed. I got my coffee and strolled off to my gate like a boss. When I sat down in my seat on the plane, and I began to settle down, something began to hit me. My impatience just cost me $10. Seems like a small price to pay in the grand scheme of things, but I wonder what else my waiting problem has cost me?

When I'm in traffic and I'm speeding and weaving all to make an appointment on time or to just get home a few minutes quicker . . . is my wait problem costing me my safety and others'?

When I'm listening to one of my kids tell me a rather lengthy story while I'm in a hurry to either say something profound or get back to a text I was writing . . . is my wait problem costing me my connection with my daughter?

When I'm at a table in a restaurant and my food is taking forever, and I am getting restless and beginning to get confrontational with the server . . . is my wait problem costing me my witness as a follower of Jesus?

When I'm trying to multitask and I'm attempting to answer a text, empty the dishwasher, tell the kids to do their homework, and talk to my wife who has something important to share—all while watching a game on TV out of the corner of my eye . . . is my attempt to get everything done quickly only accomplishing doing nothing well?

And I must admit, the same is true with my prayer life. Because I hate to wait, I overlook the reason for prayer in the first place. I get so caught up in getting what I want from God, I forget why I'm supposed to talk to God in the first place.

What is that reason? You'll have to wait.

Years ago, there was a hilarious comedy sketch on television featuring the comedian Bob Newhart. He was playing a psychologist who would see patients with severe anxiety and depression and his approach was simple. They'd tell him what they were scared of, and he'd say, "Stop it." They'd push back, and he'd just start yelling, "Stop it!" If you've never seen it, it's worth Googling. (After you finish this chapter, of course.)

Most of the time when we get impatient with God, we either blame God or blame ourselves. We tell him to hurry up, or we tell ourselves to get over it. Stop it! But it's bigger than that. There is something we can do that can turn our wandering in the wilderness into walking with God.

It was a practice that the nation of Israel had to learn. Sure, they had some pretty big answers to prayer: deliverance from Egypt, crossing the Red Sea, manna from heaven, water from a rock, all the judges who rescued them, all the battles they won, the eventual arrival of the Messiah. But have you ever thought about how long they had to wait for some of these?

They waited over four hundred years to be delivered from slavery.

They waited forty years to get into the Promised Land.

They waited forty years for each judge to save them.

They waited four hundred years for the Messiah.

I struggle with forty minutes. Who am I kidding? I struggle with forty seconds.

Part of This Waiting Struggle Is Due to Our Culture

We live in a "buy now" world. With one click, we can have the product delivered to our door the next day. And if it's two to three days later, it feels like an eternity. We no longer have to go to a video store to rent a movie and pray that they have a copy left; we just download on our phone immediately. We can have food delivered to our door. We can have instant almost every-thing. And we expect God to be on demand as well.

So, when we pray, it is natural for us to be impatient.

Now, here's my problem with prayer, and maybe this is yours as well: If it takes so long, if sometimes the answer is no, and if in some cases he's going to do what he wants anyway . . . Why even bother? Why pray?

Haven't you wondered that before? Isn't that what we all think when it seems our prayers don't get past the ceiling? Why even bother with all this?

When I pray for the family in our church whose mom is dying of cancer and she still dies, naturally they ask me: "I prayed, nothing happened. Why bother?" And I wonder the same thing.

When I pray for my struggle with diabetes or my gen-eral anxiety disorder to be taken away and it is not, I wonder, why bother?

When I pray for my daughters to not suffer from these same afflictions and yet they still fight anxiety, I wonder, why bother?

And maybe that's why you picked up this book. You want to know what to do while you wait, but what you're really won-dering is, *Is there a magic formula I'm missing?* And if there is not, then why bother?

Let's be honest, aren't there times when you pray that you're just glad it's done? Like eating oatmeal. You know it's good for you, but you don't really enjoy it. I think this is what C. S. Lewis was getting at when he called prayer "irksome." Sometimes it's so frustrating and seems so empty that you just wonder, what's the point?

This had to be on the minds of the people who hung out with Jesus. They had prayed for four hundred years for a Messiah, and nothing. Do you think that some of them had given up? They had prayed to be free from Roman oppression . . . and still nothing. Do you think that they were wondering, why bother?

So, when Jesus launches into the Sermon on the Mount, he says, "When you pray, don't babble on and on as the Gentiles do. They think their prayers are answered merely by repeating their words again and again. Don't be like them, for your Father knows exactly what you need even before you ask him!" (Matt. 6:7–8 NLT).

Huh? If God already knows exactly what we need, then why even bother?

But before he can field all their raised hands and confused looks, Jesus says, speaking of prayer, when you pray, "Pray like this: Our Father."

This would have been even more shocking than "he already knows." Wait, did you just say *our* Father? I've heard you call him Father before, but now you are telling us to talk about him that way as well? To talk to him as *our* Father?

Keep in mind this was in a culture that feared saying the name of God. A culture that assumed the only ones who could talk to God were the religious leaders. And those leaders weren't Jesus's audience. His audience that day was used to fishing all day and getting nothing, trying to raise a family under Roman rule, begging God to keep their animals healthy, going to the temple every year with sacrifices and hoping God would grant forgiveness, and after years of silence and seeming inactivity they are wondering, why bother. Now, this holy man from Nazareth has told them to call God "our Father"?

Jesus is changing the way they viewed prayer.

From have to . . . to get to.

From a list . . . to a love.

From a religion . . . to a relationship.

God is our Father and like a father, sometimes he says yes, sometimes he says no, but he always values the conversation.

Family vacations for us have always been a big deal. And many times, we do them by car. We'll drive for hours at a time, and many times it ends up like the movie *Vacation*. While in the car, the kids will start asking for things. "Can we stop soon?" "Dad, I saw a sign for the world's largest ball of string; can we stop?" "Look, there's a Cracker Barrel; can we stop?" (Okay, maybe that one was me.) And sometimes my answer is, "YES! Let's do it!" And sometimes my answer is, "No, we need to keep going." And sometimes my wife's answer is, "Yes, but just to use the bathroom; then we are back on the road." I would hate it if my kids reduced that entire trip down to "Dad said no" or "I didn't get to see the ball of string because we were in a hurry to get to a theme park." Because my memories are not of the nos, but of the time together. The laughs and even the tears in the car. The jokes. The funny moments that we'll never forget. The joy was in the journey. The ride was about the relationship.

I had a chance to interview prolific author and teacher Jan Johnson on my podcast. Since she has written multiple books on prayer and serves as a spiritual director for many, I decided to ask her why we should bother. If God knows what we need already, and in some cases it seems like his mind is already made up, why pray? Her answer was simple but profound: "The question we all have to wrestle with when it comes to why bother with prayer is 'Is God enough, or do we need his stuff too?'"

In her book *When the Soul Listens,* about contemplative prayer, she pushes back against the step-by-step approach that many Christians prescribe for prayer, and instead says, "The contemplative approach isn't so much about *doing* these practices as about *living with Christ in the midst of them* so that they shape my life with God" (emphasis mine). She goes on to emphasize God's *presence* in people's lives, instead of setting aside compartmentalized time with God in prayer. She says, "The stillness of contemplative prayer helps make us aware that God is truly with us and allows us to hear when God chooses to nudge, guide, direct, or even challenge us." When God is *present* with people, they should be ready for an adventure: "[A contemplative] life involves surprising and intriguing adventures."

Perhaps me getting my prayers answered was never the point.

Jan was a student of Dallas Willard, and her words directed me to his work *Hearing God.* It sounds like this is what he was driving at as well: "In the union and communion of the believer with God, their two beings are unified and inhabit each other."

Willard even compares the relationship between person and God with the relationship between two people. He writes, "[God] speaks with us individually as it is appropriate—which is only to be expected between persons who know one another, care about each other and are engaged in common enterprises."

Willard will take it even a step further. He cautions us against just begging God for his stuff, and instead encourages begging God for his voice. Many seem stuck in their relationship with God because they are busy trying to get answers about what to do in certain situations. Willard's emphasis on friendship and union, then, is the basis to his perspective on prayer. "Learning to hear God," Willard explains "is much more about becoming comfortable in a continuing conversation" than "turning God into an ATM for advice, or treating the Bible as a crystal ball." Even though waiting on God can seem excruciating at times, it is in these moments that we can find the deepest levels of friendship and support from the Spirit.

I remember when I was first diagnosed with diabetes. I was away at college and my parents called to give me the results of some recent blood work. My excessive weight loss and thirst were symptoms of a deeper issue. My pancreas had shut down and I was now a type 1 diabetic.

My mind was filled with questions. What does this mean? Can I grow out of it? Is there medication to fix this? The one thing I knew was that I had to drive three hours back to my home and be admitted to the hospital. I told my friends what was going on and that I was headed back, and they stopped me: "We'll drive you." My mind was filled with complications. Why would you do this? How are you getting back? How can this help? All of which they talked me out of. "We are driving you."

I can tell you this. Not one of them was a doctor or even training to be one. Not one of them had a clue what diabetes was or how it would impact my life. But they had the one thing I needed: friendship. I was not alone. They couldn't fix me; but in the end, their friendship sustained me. I was glad they bothered.

Richard Foster explains that this time with God in prayer wraps people in the Father's love. He says, "[In prayer,] we allow ourselves to be gathered up into the arms of the Father and let him sing his love song over us." This is why we bother.

Oswald Chambers, in his devotional masterpiece, states, "God does not tell you what He is going to do—He reveals to you who He is." He argues that prayer is not as much about petition–reception; it is about entering into a relationship with God. Perhaps the reason we keep praying is to keep building on a relationship with God that he initiated, he perfects, and he fulfills.

Jan Johnson continues by explaining that asking God questions is not as important as pursuing the act of being present with God. When talking about waiting to hear answers from God, she says, "I no longer need to know the answer because I better know the Answerer." Similarly, she states, "Asking God questions involves waiting for an answer, which is a problem only if you're asking only for utilitarian purposes—to get what you want *now.* But when we understand that we live in union with God, waiting means you already have what you ultimately want—life with God."

I learned this slowly last year.

As I looked through my journal, I kicked off the year with a prayer for our church that was very common for the first of the year: "God, please walk with us this year through whatever may come. Praying for a great year for our church and staff." Little did I know I was walking into the most turbulent time in ministry for our church, our community, and me. It began with the revelation of a moral failure on staff. That, coupled with his history of mental disorder, ended with his suicide. This was devastating to our church, our team, and especially me. We had been friends for years. "God, where are you? Where's the great year I prayed for?" Just when it seemed to be getting back to normal, wildfires broke out over the summer and threatened our entire valley. Our family was one of the many who were evacuated. Some families lost their homes. "God, why now? Didn't we talk about this?" Not long after this, one of our local high schools experienced a school shooting. A troubled young man brought a gun to school one day and shot five other students, killing two of them and then himself. Three of the victims attended our church, including one who passed away. Suddenly, national news came calling and it seemed the entire city was asking, "Why?" and "Where is God?" I believe I was asking the same thing. Ten days after this horrific event, a good friend of our family, one of the earliest members of our church, lost her battle with cancer at the young age of fifty-one. At this point, I have to admit . . . the idea of my shallow optimistic prayer at the beginning of the year seemed unheard.

As I was reflecting on the year, my mind was drawn to a text message I received months earlier from a friend. It directed my attention to a verse written by Jeremiah, often called the "weeping prophet." After the destruction of Jerusalem, he writes these words:

> I will never forget this awful time, as I grieve over my loss. Yet I still dare to hope when I remember this: The faithful love of the LORD never ends! His mercies never cease. Great is his faithfulness; his mercies begin afresh each morning. I say to myself, "The LORD is my inheritance; therefore, I will hope in him!" (Lam. 3:20–24 NLT)

As I began to look through my journal and reflect on the year, I began to notice the mercies that were fresh every morning: The love of my family. The unity of our church.

The opportunities to serve the community. An unexpected text from a friend. A surprise visit from a personal hero. An uncommon strength in tough times. Stories of conversions at the funeral and prayer vigils. The quiet assurance that I was not alone. Somehow, over the course of the heaviest year of my life, I sensed the lightness and support that can only come from the closeness of my heavenly Father. A closeness that gave me confidence in comforting grieving family members and a shocked community.

My relationship with my God felt more like time with my Father, rather than obeying my God. He walked with me and guided me, even when everything didn't turn out the way I wanted.

Now that I think about it, this is exactly what Jesus did to answer my prayers.

Discussion Questions

1. Are you the talkative one in relationships?

2. How often do you wonder, "Why bother?" When it comes to prayer?

3. Do you tend to go silent with God for long periods of time?

4. What do you tell your kids if they ask, "Why pray?"

5. If praying is about a conversation, what do you need to do more of . . . talking or listening?

Next Steps

1. "Waste" some time with God this week just recognizing he is with you.

2. Listen to my conversation with Jan Johnson on *The Rusty George Podcast*, Episode 89: "How to hear from God when you pray."

12

How Jesus Waited

You would never trust a nervous pilot.

As I write this, I'm sitting on a plane and watching the captain say hi to everyone who boards. He's smiling, he's confident, and he's ready to go. It occurred to me that I'd be rather concerned if he was sweating, trembling, and asking the passengers to pray for him. I might skip that flight and take my chances on another one.

I grew up with a neighbor who had his pilot's license. He offered to take us all for a ride one time, but my dad said, "Not until I see you fly." My dad was not a pilot. I'm not sure what he was looking for, but he stood on a runway of a private airfield and watched as our friend took off, did a couple of flybys, and then landed. I guess he wanted to see . . . was he nervous?

Waiting on God can be a nerve-racking time. But does it have to be?

One of the things about Jesus that makes me marvel is the faith he has in his Father. It's one thing to put our faith *in* Jesus; it's another to have the faith *of* Jesus. The Son of God trusts his Father and shows us how to do the same. Even when he waits. Jesus was never nervous about his Father. Even when his Father seemed silent.

We've covered seven things Jesus tells us to do while we wait.

But what does Jesus do while he waits? I think we assume that just because Jesus was God in the flesh, he had no questions for his Father or curiosity while he waited. But in the twenty-four hours leading up to his crucifixion, we see Jesus struggle with this, and he models for us what to do when God seems silent, or worse, says no.

When God Seems Silent

It's the night before Jesus is crucified and it appears everything is getting more intense. The disciples are unaware, but they do know that this Passover feast seems a bit different than the last two they've spent with Jesus. They appear to be meeting in a room they have not used before. Jesus washed their feet when they entered, and now they all feel a bit awkward. Like when your spouse sneezes and someone else says bless you before you do. They all must have been thinking, *Why didn't I think of that?* Peter got scolded, Judas ran out of the room, and then Jesus drops a "new command" on them. This was unheard of. Even if you were a rabbi, you were not the one to give a new command. That was a God thing to do. But Jesus drops all their jaws when he says, "A new command I give you: Love one another. As I have loved you, so you must love one another" (John 13:34). To be clear, the disciples are a bit confused.

Then, Jesus starts to pray. His most intimate conversation with the Father that they have heard. In fact, it's so personal, it appears that Jesus isn't even thinking about them being there. He prays for many things in this prayer, but one in particular seems to go unanswered.

> Now I am departing from the world; they are staying in this world, but I am coming to you. Holy Father, you have given me your name; now protect them by the power of your name so that they will be united just as we are. . . . I'm not asking you to take them out of the world, but to keep them safe from the evil one. (John 17:11, 15 NLT)

Jesus asks the Father for his disciples to remain united . . . just as much as the Father, Son, and Holy Spirit are united. This is an unbreakable bond. This is a glory-deferring, selfless-focused, team-first unity that is unprecedented.

Jesus prays for the disciples to be protected from the evil one. To be shielded by the hand of his Father so that the enemy who appears to be winning over Jesus will not gain any ground over his followers. But over the course of the next few hours, they seem to be anything but that.

One will betray Jesus. Another will deny knowing Jesus three separate times. And the rest will scatter, running for their lives. Anything but unified and protected. Wouldn't these be prayers you'd think the father would say yes to?

In the past, he's prayed for fish and loaves to multiply, and they did. He's asked for Lazarus to come forth, and he did. Now, he gets silence.

In *Waiting: Finding Hope When God Seems Silent*, Ben Patterson writes, "To wait with grace requires two cardinal virtues: humility and hope." He acknowledges that patience and perseverance seem like the virtues people should exercise when forced to wait, but they are secondary to humility and hope, which are the virtues that are needed to wait with grace. This is exactly what Jesus did.

When Judas shows up in the garden and betrays Jesus with a kiss . . . Jesus shows humility and hope. When Jesus looks across the courtyard only to hear Peter deny knowing him for the third time . . . he shows humility and hope. And when they scatter and he's left alone, he is never nervous . . . he has humility and hope.

How does Jesus wait? With humility that his Father has a bigger plan. With hope that one day the disciples will be unified and the evil one will be defeated.

Dallas Willard reminds us in *Life without Lack* that Paul's admonition to take every thought captive and submit it to Christ (2 Cor. 10:5) "involves us beginning to think about God as Jesus thought about him, and to trust God as Jesus trusted him—moving from having faith *in* Jesus to having the faith *of* Jesus" (emphasis original).

But that is just when his Father is silent. What about when he says no?

I've asked this question many times in my life, but never more than in the past year. Racing to the hospital after a school shooting while praying, "Please, God, let her live." Walking with a family where a forty-nine-year-old woman in seemingly good health just got a death sentence in the form of cancer, all the while praying, "God, please heal her!" And then COVID-19 hits. "Please, God, take this away." "Please, God, let our churches gather for Easter." "Please, God, end the suffering." All these prayers seemed to fall on deaf ears. But forty days into our COVID-19 season, death seemed to knock on the door once more. My sister called and said that Tim, her fifty-one-year-old husband, was going in for quintuple bypass surgery. *What? He's healthy. He works out. He's young. Seriously?* My prayers went on full court press. "God, please help this surgery work." I prayed with Tim on the phone. We were all prayed up and faithed up. And the surgery went great. He was doing so well he went home early. Five days later, he received a great checkup. Then, two days later, he went into cardiac arrest in the middle of the night and never woke up. The theme song of the church during the season of COVID-19 had been "Way Maker," and we all wondered: Where was this "way maker, miracle worker, promise keeper, light in the darkness?" God was not just silent. God had said no. But why? I needed more than faith *in* Jesus—I needed the faith *of* Jesus.

When God Says No

Soon after this prayer ends and the dinner is concluded, Jesus and the disciples make the trip from inside Jerusalem to outside the city to the garden of Gethsemane on the Mount of Olives. This time, Jesus begins to pray another prayer to the Father.

He knows the end is near. He knows he's running out of time. And the humanity of Jesus has never been so intense. He withdraws from the group and begins to cry out to his Father:

> He told them, "My soul is crushed with grief to the
> point of death. Stay here and keep watch with me." He
> went on a little farther and bowed with his face to the
> ground, praying, "My Father! If it is possible, let this
> cup of suffering be taken away from me. Yet I want
> your will to be done, not mine." (Matt. 26:38–39 NLT)

The imagery is so rich. They are in a place where olives are crushed in a press for their oil, and now Jesus says to his friends, "My soul is crushed."

Ever spent a sleepless night dreading the next day? So has Jesus.

Ever felt overwhelmed like you can't go on? So has Jesus.

Ever cried out to God and wondered if he'd change his mind? So has Jesus.

In these moments when we cry out to him, he doesn't say, "Oh, that sounds awful," but rather, "I remember." The agony continues: "Then Jesus left them a second time and prayed, 'My Father! If this cup cannot be taken away unless I drink it, your will be done'" (Matt. 26:42 NLT).

Again, he cries out to his Father. This time, his praying is so intense that an eyewitness comments that he's sweating blood. This is an actual condition known as hematidrosis. It is a condition in which capillary blood vessels that feed the sweat glands rupture, causing them to exude blood, occurring under conditions of extreme physical or emotional stress.

What's fascinating about this is that many of us think our prayers are not being heard because we are not praying with enough intensity. Maybe we need to stand more, kneel more, fall on our face more. Perhaps we are not praying loud enough, or earnestly enough, or often enough. Yet, Jesus is so intense that he's sweating blood, and his father still says no.

On my first trip to Israel, I was deeply moved by standing in the garden of Gethsemane. When you stand there, you can look over the Kidron Valley into the city of Jerusalem and see the city gates and streets. At night, it would have been easy to see from the garden into the city where soldiers were gathering with torches and to hear the clanging of their swords. This means while Jesus was praying, he could have seen the soldiers gathering. In other words, while he was praying for God to say yes to his request, he could literally see God answering no.

The soldiers were coming. There would be no other options. Jesus would have to drink from this cup.

In *Waiting on God*, Charles F. Stanley encourages Christians in their expectant waiting on God by outlining a four-step process. He clearly delineates this process in the last few pages of his book: "First, humble yourself before the Lord and focus on Him rather than your desire. . . . Second, remain obedient to God's will. . . . Third, have faith that the Father will do as He has promised. . . . Finally, be courageous."

This is exactly what Jesus does. But how? How does Jesus seemingly so easily walk forward in obedience despite God's silence and then an answer of no? With courageous humility and hope.

When the No Seems Unbearable

Jesus is arrested, and then the true agony begins. He is dragged from one court to another. He is mocked, spit upon, beaten, and flogged. They slam a crown of thorns on his head, force him to carry his cross, and then nail him to it. He's been up all night, beaten to within an inch of his life, and now nailed to a tree. And it's in this moment that he cries out to God.

"At noon, darkness fell across the whole land until three o'clock. At about three o'clock, Jesus called out with a loud voice, *'Eli, Eli, lema sabachthani?'* which means 'My God, my God, why have you abandoned me?'" (Matt. 27:45–46 NLT).

Notice the distance in Jesus's voice. Normally, it's "Father," but now it's "My God, my God." This is actually the first line of a psalm Jesus would have grown up reading: "My God, my God, why have you abandoned me? Why are you so far away when I groan for help? Every day I call to you, my God, but you do not answer. Every night I lift my voice, but I find no relief" (Ps. 22:1–2 NLT).

Surely this is how he felt. Abandoned. What we forget is the next verse: "Yet you are holy, enthroned on the praises of Israel" (Ps. 22:3 NLT). You are holy. In other words, your decisions are always right. Even when they seem unbearable. Don't think Jesus didn't know the entire psalm.

Jerry Sittser experienced unbearable loss. In *A Grace Disguised*, he tells how in one car accident, he lost his mother, his wife, and their daughter. In one moment, his life was devastated. He would pray every day, like most of us, for his family's safety. Now, why were they gone? Why was he still here? Why would this happen? Over the months ahead, he confesses he didn't even pray. He couldn't. How could he even begin to talk to the God who would allow such a thing?

Isn't this what we all want to know? If you're good . . . how could you let this happen?

This is what my friend Bryan wants to know. His daughter was one of the victims of the Saugus High School shooting. In a matter of eight seconds, the shooter injured three students, killing two of them, Dominick and Gracie, and then turned the gun on himself.

Gracie and her family go to our church. In one of our many conversations, they wanted to know what most of us are asking: Why?

Why did God allow this boy to do this?

Why did some live and not others?

Was Gracie chosen to die?

Why couldn't the gun just jam and no one get hurt?

Why would God allow any of this?

Jerry Sittser wanted to know this as well. And what began to help him was looking at the story of Job and the story of Joseph.

Job was a man who lost everything as well. In a short period of time, Job loses his children, his home, and his wealth. When he turns to his wife for support, she simply says, "Are you still maintaining your integrity? Curse God and die!" (Job 2:9). Slowly, Job starts asking questions of God, like we all would. Why? Where were you? How could you? Why me? God patiently lets Job get it all off his chest, and then God steps in. And when the questions stop, the awe and wonder begin.

Joseph, on the other hand, is given a dream from God, but has to wait for it to come to fruition. He suffers rejections from his brothers, being sold into slavery and wrongfully accused and imprisoned. Yet, despite all seeming lost and being far from home, it turns out he is exactly where God wanted him to be: Egypt. Now, he is in a position to be summoned by Pharaoh and eventually be put in charge. God used the wondering and the pain to bring about the fulfillment of the dream.

How Jesus Dealt with the Silence

Thomas Smail wrote about what Jesus was going through in the garden of Gethsemane, and how he was able to trust God in the midst of his pain. It helped me understand something important about trusting God.

> The Father that Jesus addresses in the garden is the one that he has known all his life and found to be bountiful in his provision, reliable in his promises and utterly faithful in his love. He can obey the will that sends him to the cross with hope and expectation because it is the will of Abba whose love has been so proved that it can now be trusted so fully by being obeyed so completely. This is not legal obedience driven by commandment, but trusting response to known love.

How did Jesus make it? How did he press on in the silence? To just say he was God in the flesh is to discount his humanity. The way Jesus was able to deal with the silence from his Father was because he knew the heart of his Father. He knew he could trust him through the pain. He had walked with him so closely for all of eternity—and specifically the last thirty-three years on earth—and he knows that silence is not an indictment on his Father's character.

Through Jesus trusting his Father, I find it easier to trust him as well. When I encounter school shootings, tornadoes, child predators, drunk driving accidents, and stillbirths, even though I can't make sense of it, I can trust my heavenly Father because Jesus did. God is still great. God is still good. And in the end, everything can and will be redeemed.

This was the conclusion that Jerry Sittser eventually came to. "So we ponder and pray. We move toward God, then away from him. We wrestle in our souls to believe. Finally, we choose God, and in the choosing we learn that he has already chosen us and has already been drawing us to him." Even after such pain, struggle, and suffering, Sittser's writing echoes the apostle Paul in saying, "Pain and death do not have the final word; God does."

Furthermore, he says, "I have grieved long and hard and intensely. But I have found comfort knowing that the sovereign God, who is in control of everything, is the same God who has experienced the pain I live with every day."

Father Damien was a priest who became famous for his willingness to serve lepers. He moved to Kalawao—a village on the island of Molokai, in Hawaii, that had been quarantined to serve as a leper colony.

For sixteen years, he lived with them. He learned to speak their language. He bandaged their wounds, met their needs when others stayed away, and preached to hearts that would otherwise have been left alone. He organized schools, bands, and choirs. He built homes so that the lepers could have shelter. He built two thousand coffins by hand so that when they died, they could be buried with dignity.

Slowly, it was said, Kalawao became a place to live rather than a place to die, for Father Damien offered hope.

Father Damien was not careful about keeping his distance. He did nothing to separate himself from his people. He ate with them, fed them, and even shared his pipe with them. And after years of living this close to them, he became like them.

One Sunday, he stood up in the church to deliver a sermon, and he began with these two words: "We lepers . . ." He was no longer just helping them; he was now one of them. He had chosen to live as they lived; now, eventually, he would die as they died. But they would do so together.

When Jesus left this earth, he began his message: "We lepers . . ." He was no longer apart from us; he was one of us. He was no longer watching us; he was walking with us. And because of this, Jesus knows what it's like to be human. He knows what it's like to pray and hear silence. He knows what it's like to wait. When we face the waiting . . . when we feel the silence after amen . . . Jesus doesn't say, "That sounds bad," or, "I'll comfort you," but rather, "I remember."

I remember what it's like to wait.

I remember what it's like to dread the next day.

I remember just how long a night can be.

I remember what it's like to lose a friend.

I remember what it's like to bury a parent.

I remember what it's like to be betrayed.

I remember what it's like to feel abandoned.

I remember what it's like to cry out to heaven and hear silence.

And I can tell you . . . you can trust your Father.

Discussion Questions

1. Have you ever had to trust someone who was nervous?

2. How does Jesus's experience in the garden inform how you pray?

3. What does Jesus's response to God's silence teach you?

4. How does it make you feel to know Jesus has asked God, "Where have you gone?"

5. How does it make you feel to know Jesus can sympathize and empathize in your struggle?

Next Steps

1. Courageously wait with humility and hope.

Thank you for reading *After Amen*. I hope it gave you hope as writing it did for me. Can I give you a free gift to say thanks?

Go to my website, pastorrustygeorge.com, and enter the promotional code "afterafteramen" for a free gift!

Thanks again!

Acknowledgments

Thank you to all who pray with me and for me:
The Real Life prayer team, our board of directors, our staff,
and all the churches of Real Life Church Ministries

Thank you to all who made this book possible:
Leafwood Publishers, Olivia Hastie, Debbie Robert,
Josh Komo, Brenda Hunten, Jason Fikes, Don Gates,
and all my heroes who endorsed this

And thank you to my holy huddle,
my in-home prayer team,
and my favorite people in the world:
Lorrie, Lindsey, and Sidney

About the Author

RUSTY GEORGE is the lead pastor of Real Life Church Ministries—multisite churches in ministries in California. He is also the author of *Better Together: Discovering the Power of Community* and *Justice.Mercy.Humility: A Simple Path to Following Jesus.* Connect with him on social media @rustylgeorge and through his website, pastorrustygeorge.com.

CPSIA information can be obtained
at www.ICGtesting.com
Printed in the USA
LVHW090146190721
693062LV00003B/156

9 781684 260812